Architectural Practice
A Critical View

Robert Gutman

Princeton Architectural Press

This publication was produced under a cooperative agreement between Robert Gutman and the Design Arts Program of the National Endowment for the Arts.

The views expressed in this publication are those of the author and do not necessarily reflect those of the National Endowment for the Arts.

Frank M. Hodsoll, Chairman
National Endowment for the Arts.

Printed by R.R. Donnelley, Harrisonburg, Virginia;
special thanks to Laura Sanders and Caren Leach

92 91 90 89   5 4 3 2

Princeton Architectural Press
37 East 7th Street
New York, NY 10003
212-995-9620

Library of Congress Cataloging-in-Publication Data
Gutman, Robert
    Architectural practice: a critical view / Robert Gutman.
    160p. 15 x 22.7cm.
    Bibliography: p.131
    Includes index.
    ISBN 0-910413-45-2 (pbk.)
    1. Architectural practice—United States. 2. Architectural
services marketing—United States. I. Title.
NA1996.G86 1988
720' .68—dc19   88-804
                                   CIP

Contents

Illustrations

Tables

Charts and Graphs

Acknowledgments

I wish to thank the Design Arts Program of the National Endowment for the Arts for its support of the project leading to the publication of this book. I appreciate especially the encouragement of Ms. Adele Chatfield-Taylor, the director of the program; and also her predecessor, Mr. Michael Pittas. At different stages I have profited from the advice and support of other members of the program staff, including Wayne Linker, Marcia Sartwell, Margot Villecco, and Charles Zucker.

This book grew out of discussions I have had for several years with professional degree students in the School of Architecture at Princeton University, who were interested in a more accurate assessment of contemporary design and building practice than studio education provides. Several Princeton students assisted me as researchers on the topics discussed in this book and in the preparation of articles cited in the bibliography, in particular Keller Easterling, Natalie Shivers, and Elizabeth Zenowich.

In preparing the manuscript for submission to the publisher, several friends and colleagues read it. They were Dana Cuff, Mary Dolden, Francis Duffy, Stephen Kieran, Kevin Lippert, and Barbara Westergaard. Although they are in no way responsible for the final version, I benefitted greatly from their comments. Like other social scientists who write about the problems of the architecture profession today, I also have learned much from the work of Judith Blau, Magali Sarfatti Larson, Roger Montgomery, and Francis Ventre.

Frances Chen provided welcome answers to many bibliographical inquiries. Barbara Westergaard displayed her usual good judgment on editorial matters. John Gutman and Elizabeth Gutman provided assistance in getting the manuscript ready for the press. Sonya Rudikoff gave invaluable advice on numerous questions involving the cultural situation of architecture. I am also grateful for the careful attention to the project by the staff of Princeton Architectural Press, especially Elizabeth Short and Ann Urban.

The statement by Le Corbusier in the epigraph is from a letter he wrote to William Ritter, May 22, 1916. It is quoted in Eleanor Gregh, "The Domino Idea," *Oppositions* 15/16 (1979), p. 77. Herbert Croly's statement is included in his article "American Artists and their Public," *Architectural Record*, 10 (1900-1901), p. 257. The lines by Kipling appear in "A Truthful Song," *Rudyard Kipling's Verse*. Garden City, N.Y.: Doubleday and Co., 1946, p. 657.

Princeton, N.J.
September 1987

"Business! What a dilemma! If you try to please people, you become corrupt and sell yourself; if you do what you feel you must do, you cause displeasure and create a void around yourself."

—Le Corbusier

The good American architects on the other hand cannot complain of being neglected. They are, rather, all too prosperous. A great many of them certainly have more work than they can do consistent with giving proper attention to the refinement and detail of their plans. The office of a prosperous architect is organized like any other great business concern, particularly for the purpose of turning out in a manner satisfactory to their clients the designs of very many, too many buildings. What is, however, worst of all, the architect rarely occupies with respect to his client a position of sufficient independence. The average American is willing to spend a good deal of money for esthetic effect, but very little for esthetic propriety; and much of a conscientious architect's energy is wasted either in bullying or persuading his client to do the right thing.

—Herbert Croly

I tell this tale, which is strictly true,
Just by way of convincing you
How very little, since things were made,
Things have altered in the building trade.

—Rudyard Kipling

Introduction

This book discusses important trends within the architectural profession and the building industry, as well as among clients and the public at large, that are leading architects to question their values, self-conceptions, and methods of practice. These developments represent a new set of conditions which, when taken together, constitute a "world" that members of the profession experience daily. The experiences shape architects' ideas about how they should act in order to realize their goals as professionals. It is because this world differs in so many respects from the ordinary professional experience of previous generations of architects that we now question traditional images of the architect.

The text discusses ten trends that have been transforming the subjective experiences of architects. They are: (1) the expanding demand for architectural services; (2) changes in the structure of the demand; (3) the oversupply, or potential oversupply, of entrants into the profession; (4) the increased size and complexity of buildings; (5) the consolidation and professionalization of the construction industry; (6) the greater rationality and sophistication of client organizations; (7) the more intense competition between architects and other professions; (8) the greater competition within the profession; (9) the continuing economic difficulties of practice; and (10) changing expectations of architecture among the public.

This book is mainly concerned with a description of these trends. However, I do refer repeatedly to the methods through which the profession is responding to the changing context, and this is the central focus of the discussion in the chapter "Challenges to Architecture."

In investigating conditions of practice I have followed several different paths simultaneously, using the research techniques that were most appropriate for specific problem-areas. For example, in dealing with the supply of architects and firms, I have mainly analyzed data collected by the Bureau of the Census, relating these data to information published by the American Institute of Architects (AIA) and the Association of Collegiate Schools of Architecture (ACSA). In considering the changes taking place in the demand for architectural services, I have relied on interviews with practitioners and clients, studies of developments in other producer service businesses, and data from biographies of architects and histories of the profession. My treatment of competition within the profession, and from other design professions, is based on material obtained from marketing experts, builders, developers, interior designers, landscape architects, and civil engineers. A good deal of the information reported in the chapter "The Public's Relation to Architecture" is based on interviews with three types of "publics": politicians and government officials, representatives of user and community groups, and critics, museum officials, and publishers.

In general, I discovered that much more data are available about architectural practice than previous studies have shown. However, the quality of these data is very uneven. In the text, I suggest some of the areas where intensive further study is needed. However, my primary aim has not been to define topics for future research. I believe that the charge originally put to me by the Arts Endowment when it undertook to sponsor this study is best served by emphasizing the facts we have now, and by indicating the implications of this information for the future of architectural practice.

My descriptions of the changed world of practice frequently differ from the assumptions in terms of which architects talk about their practices, present themselves to clients, and portray the life of an architect to their students. There are many reasons why architects, like members of other professions, cling to an outmoded or anachronistic conception of social reality. To acknowledge its true character is to shatter several myths concerning the power, freedom, and autonomy of the profession. At the same time, events of daily life and recent theories popular in the discipline disclose the force of contemporary practice all too clearly. I hope therefore, that despite the understandable inclination to promulgate an idealized version of an architectural life, most architects will recognize substantial truth in my description.

The gap between the premises and expectations of the world that architects experience subjectively, and the ideas architects carry around in their minds and espouse out of habit, is the principal reason for this book. In my view, the unreality of the espoused view of the world of practice is perpetuated by the profession itself, by the schools, and to some extent by the architectural press, and these distortions make it more difficult for architects to deal creatively and constructively with the problems which the profession faces. My hope is that by providing a text about practice which is grounded in research, this book will make it easier for the profession to liberate itself from conventional points of view and ideologies, and confront modern conditions of architecture and building in a positive light.

The Rising Demand
For Architectural Services

The demand for the services of architects and architectural firms is expanding. This is apparent from the number of small firms being started by recent graduates, the many offices of different sizes that are busily working and hiring new staff, the increasing attention being shown to architecture in the public press, the media, and educated circles; and the general excitement that permeates many different levels of the architectural community. The impression is supported by statistical data.

Although demand is expanding, it is surprising how many members of the profession believe the opposite. One reason for the persistence of pessimism is that not all firms have benefited from the general increase in work. Some established offices have actually been losing their share of the market, and are being supplanted by newer firms that are more aggressive in getting work or are in tune with the demand for specialized services or for buildings with a distinctive appearance. It is understandable that the offices that are falling behind would think that demand is shrinking. Another reason is the intense competitive effort that is required for a firm to obtain a commission. Many architects interpret the increase in competition as evidence of a contracting market. But it is wrong to conclude that because there are more firms now engaged in seeking work that the total volume of jobs available has diminished. The demands for services and competitiveness are connected trends, but the relationship is based on the fact that competition in the profession stimulates architects to work harder at marketing their skills.

A third explanation for the endurance of the negative view is that the demand for services does not result in greater control by architects over the design and building process. Indeed, as I shall discuss later on, many of the new clients reduce the architects' role to the application of specialized expertise, and deny them coordinating and supervisory responsibilities. Pessimism is also an emotion through which many architects manifest their distress about the inferior quality of the products whose construction the profession oversees. An argument can be made to support the view that the average quality of buildings being turned out now is of a higher grade than fifty years ago, and that this improvement is partly the result of the greater use of architects by public and private owners. Nevertheless, it is true that tens of thousands of buildings constructed each year are inappropriately sited, improperly scaled, ugly, badly constructed, poorly laid out, inadequately heated and ventilated, and stocked with inferior furnishings and equipment. Many of the structures with these deficiencies are the work of professional architects.

There are about 25,000 architectural offices now in the United States. Half of these are one-person offices doing minor jobs, and often run part-time by architects whose main employment is in large architectural or engineering firms. Since the reports about practice issued by the Bureau of the Census deal only with offices having at least one employee regularly on the payroll in addition to the principal, there is no official information about one-person firms.[1] Despite the absence of data about them comparable in depth to the information available about bigger offices, they represent an important tradition in the profession. Many architects prefer to practice by themselves. One-person firms frequently enter open competitions, and often generate innovative architectural concepts and ideas. This is the kind of firm that is most familiar to the typical client who wants a garage converted or an office space renovated. To the extent that these practices are run by men and women who moonlight from other jobs, or who derive their main income from teaching, they are sometimes economically viable.

The other 12,000 firms, which range in size from one employee in addition to the principal to offices with several hundred employees, are more representative of the direction in which practice is moving.[2] It is these offices that are responding to the changing conditions discussed in what follows. By concerning themselves with problems of marketing, management, and alternative strategies of practice, these firms are setting the pace for the development of the profession in the future. However, one should be aware that most of the 12,000, although they have moved beyond the one-person type, are still small offices, especially when compared to the organizations of their clients. One-half of these 12,000 firms have fewer than five employees, including technicians and non-professional staff. Over 90 percent have fewer than twenty employees. An office of ten persons altogether, perhaps only seven of whom are architects, can be designing buildings for a university or a commercial establishment that employs thousands. This imbalance in size between architect and

1. Robert Gutman, Barbara Westergaard, and David Hicks, "The Structure of Design Firms," p. 3.

2. Size is a useful variable for distinguishing types of practice because it is highly correlated with other critical features of an office and its work: the scale of projects, job complexity, the degree of specialization of the firm, management structure, pay levels, commitment to professional values, and so on. See Dana Cuff, *The Social Construction of Design*, chap. 2.

client, and also architect and contractor, is possible because of the nature of architectural design as a type of work activity. However, the discrepancy in size is also the basis for many obstacles to the architect becoming the controlling voice in building projects.

Like the one-person firm, the small office is another example of traditional architectural practice. The new features of the current group of small offices is that there are many more of them, their average size is bigger, and their activities are conducted with greater attention to criteria of good management and profitability. The more unusual feature of the present structure of practice is the emergence of close to 250 firms with over fifty employees. A few offices of this size were famous in earlier periods and produced a tremendous volume of buildings and plans, including Burnham and Co. and McKim, Mead and White in the 1890s and Albert Kahn's organization in the 1920s, but these were exceptions. The very large firms of the present are a phenomenon that emerged following World War II.

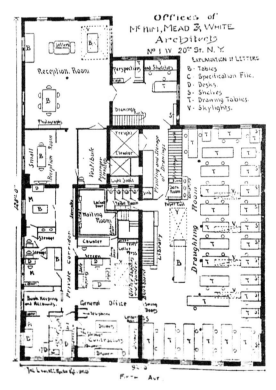

Figure 1. Floor plan of the office of McKim, Mead and White, 1 West 20th Street, New York City, 1891. According to Leland M. Roth, during this period the size of the firm reached a high of 110, because of the extra work connected with the Columbian Exposition.

Figure 2. The staff of the firm headed by Albert Kahn, Detroit, 1924. Kahn himself is marked number 1. The office had about 250 professional, technical, and secretarial staff, of whom more than 50 were absent on vacation or supervising jobs when the photograph was taken. It was the largest architectural office the world had ever known. The Fisher building, designed by Kahn and then under constuction, can be seen in the background.

They represent the advance edge along which growth in the profession is taking place, and they dominate the market for architectural services. In the ten year period between 1972 and 1982, for example, all firms with employees increased in number by 20 percent, while firms with over fifty on the staff rose by about 50 percent (table 1). The 250 big firms, which constitute only 2 percent of all the architectural firms in the country, collect 30 percent of the fees for architectural services. The other 11,750 offices divide the remaining 70 percent of the receipts (table 2 and chart 1).

Within the group of 250 offices with fifty or more employees, there are several enormous firms. Good examples of this type are Helmuth, Obata and Kassabaum in St. Louis; HKS in Dallas; Cooper, Carry and Associates in Atlanta; and John Portman Associates, also in Atlanta. These firms rank second, third, fourth, and fifth in the nation according to the volume of space they designed in 1986. The four firms together designed 70 million square feet of building space with a total value of 4.25 billion dollars. The four firms each have several offices in addition to their home base. The number of employees in each firm averages 440, of whom 240 are architects, 20 are landscape architects, and 45 are interior designers.[3]

The growth in receipts of architecture firms can be taken as an indication of expanding demand. In the ten-year period between 1972

3. "The 200 Architectural Giants of 1986," p. 38.

and 1982, the total annual receipts of the offices covered by the census reports increased from a little over 2 billion dollars to almost 6 billion, an increase, when corrected for inflation, of 25 percent. These data are based on receipts from both domestic and overseas projects. The increase was greatest in the larger firms, those with 100 or more employees. The receipts of the average firm in this group increased from $5.6 million in 1972 to $15 million ten years later. Adjusted for inflation, this represented a rise of approximately 15 percent. The average receipts of the small firms, those with 20 or fewer employees increased by a smaller amount, and when corrected for the decline in the value of the dollar, actually decreased.[4]

The annual billings of the top 500 design firms included in surveys published by *Engineering News Record* each year indicate similar trends. In 1964, for example, *ENR* reported total design billings that were only 13 percent of 1984's volume, total professional design staff was less than a third of 1984 staff, and only three firms posted billings of more than $10 million. By 1985 the survey boasted over 200 firms with at least $10 million in billings and 17 firms with billings of $100 million or more.[5] The *ENR* survey covers engineering and architecture firms (EA) as well as firms that confine their work to architecture alone (A) or sell engineering services but make architecture predominant (AE). The billings of EA firms are the largest of all design firms because they design bridges, tunnels and other private and public utilities, in addition to buildings. As a result, the *ENR* billings usually show better results for the design professions than the census data I have cited, which cover only architecture firms.[6]

An even more revealing indicator of the growth in demand is that the architect's share of every dollar spent on construction is increasing. For example, between 1972 and 1982, the ratio of the receipts of architectural firms to the total receipts of the companies that construct buildings increased by almost one-third, from $2.00 per $100 expended on building construction to $2.70 per $100.[7]

4. The sources for these conclusions are U.S. Department of Commerce, Bureau of the Census, *Census, Census of Service Industries for 1972 and 1982.*

5. "500 Growth Suffers a Few Setbacks," *ENR* , May 16, 1985, p. 61.

6. Again, the trends based on data comparing 1964 with 1984 or 1985 information must be corrected to take inflation into account.

7. These values are derived from a comparison of receipts of architectural firms, published in the Census of Service Industries, with information about the receipts of construction companies, available in the Census of the Construction Industries. See U.S. Department of Commerce, Bureau of the Census, *Census of the Construction Industries* for the relevant years, tables 12 and 8 in the summary volumes. The data reported for architecture firms are confined to firms with a payroll, and thus exclude the very small, one-person practices.

The trends indicated by these data are consistent with informal information available about the building industry. Clients and contractors are making greater use of professional advisers to deal with their programming, management, and marketing problems. The use of experts reflects the tremendous building programs of some clients. In 1985, the five top industrial companies in the United States, IBM, International Paper, AT&T, General Motors, and United Technologies, put in place construction valued at about $1.5 billion.[8] In 1984, IBM alone erected 2.3 million square feet of office, manufacturing, and laboratory space.[9] It is understandable that when such expenditure levels are commonplace, organizations would press to achieve maximum precision in estimating the costs of construction and the expense of maintaining these facilities. They also must try to anticipate, before the building is constructed, the reactions of prospective tenants and users. The search for knowledgeable experts is forced upon them by the careful scrutiny all building projects receive now from local, state and federal authorities, to ascertain their conformity to building, environmental, safety, and health regulations. When one realizes that for the top five industrials, 70 percent of the design work is done outside the client's organization, one gets some sense of their *potential* impact on the market for architectural services. Not all of this work is available for private architectural or architectural and engineering firms, since some of it goes to construction firms, package dealers, and other groups in the building industry that are now in the business of providing architectural services.[10]

It is the view of Andrew Saint, one of the leading historians of the profession, that pressure from the client has been mainly responsible for the successive definitions of the scope of architecture and the architect's role. He points out, for example, that in the period 1820 to 1850, architects found they had much more work than ever

8. Before the American automobile industry went into its decline, General Motors ran an architectural firm, Argonaut, which designed many of the company's factories and occasionally sold services to other clients. Argonaut still exists as a subsidiary of General Motors. However, its principal function now is to oversee the company's real estate operations.

9. Information about the amount of building space constructed annually by major American companies is available in estimate form in *Building Design and Construction*, December 1985.

10. I have not been able to find data that indicate the distribution of the work of the major client organizations in the private sector among the different types of businesses that purvey architectural and design services. I did contact a sample of large corporations directly, but they were unwilling to disclose the information. Almost all expenditures for design work by government departments are allocated to private offices.

before, it became easier to make a living, and the ranks of the profession expanded. Many architects of the period attributed the new security to the rise of public interest in art and propaganda for art. Saint, however, believes that the expansion was the result instead of two other developments: the explosion in the number and complexity of building types and the growth in building regulations. The effect of both these events was to require clients to seek the advice of knowledgeable experts, which in turn led architecture to pursue the path of specialization that characterizes the response to the growing demand today.[11] A similar quest, sparked by progress in sanitary legislation and the burgeoning of factory, commercial, and institutional building in the decades following the end of the Civil War, underlay the professionalization of architectural practice in the United States. Diana Balmori has shown that professionalization meant in this context the development of practices utilizing a division of labor, allowing the design architect who ran the firm to work on more than one building at a time. The office of the New York architect George Post was one of the earliest to employ this method of organization, enabling Post to operate with a permanent staff of twenty-one people as early as 1875. Post was pressed to conduct his practice this way in order to cope with the demands of clients, such as Western Union Telegraph, who were constructing the first round of a building type that soon was to become familiar to architects, the headquarters building.[12]

In the lexicon of macroeconomic analysis, architectural practice is classified as a producer service business, since the bulk of practice today provides services to producers of commodities (manufacturers) and to other service businesses rather than to the final consumer.[13] The major producer service businesses fall into two categories: those, including advertising and public relations, that are mainly commercial and whose staffs, although they require advanced education, do not require specialized training; and those run and staffed by men and women with professional degrees. Along with architecture, the professional producer services include accounting, engineering, law, management consulting, and scientific research. This latter group is, when measured by the increase in the size of its labor force, and its share of GNP, the fastest growing of all service businesses. Its growth is tied to the expansion of the highly

11. Andrew Saint, *The Image of the Architect*, pp. 66-68.

12. Diana Balmori, "George B. Post: The Process of Design and the New American Architectural Office (1868-1913)," pp. 348-355.

13. For a discussion of the characteristics of architectural practices that make it useful to regard them as a service industry, see my paper, "Architecture as a Service Industry."

rationalized industry that is the dominant source of economic expansion in advanced nations, including the United States.

The favorable situation in which architecture now finds itself is a function in part of the behavior of the category of modern business enterprise to which it belongs. In the American economy today many companies have exhausted most of the possibilities for efficiencies in the production of goods, despite the new emphasis on "competitiveness." As a consequence, even the manufacturing sector is now looking for ways to lower costs and thus raise profits by examining techniques for making administrative and service functions more efficient. Architectural services fit this ambition to the extent that the skills of architects can contribute to reducing the cost of constructing and maintaining facilities, including plants and buildings. The search for economies is not limited to the industrial sector but extends to the non-profit institutions of government, education and the church.[14]

The producer service function can also be handled in-house, by clients hiring their own architects. There has been substantial growth in this type of employment since World War II. For example, between 1960 and 1980, the number of architects employed outside private architectural or engineering firms increased from five to twenty thousand (see table 7). A large portion of this group was working for clients or client representatives. In 1982, according to the rosters of the AIA, 2,300 AIA members were working for federal, state and municipal governments and more than 500 architects were in industry. The number of registered architects in the government and industry categories together is probably double this number.[15] In the New York region alone in 1986, there were over 550 registered architects working for 52 government agencies, and the AIA chapter there estimated that 40 percent of all architecture in the region is carried out by members of the profession working in these agencies.[16]

In the housing industry, staff architects design tens of thousands of units each year. According to a survey of the 300 largest owners and developers of buildings in the United States conducted in 1985 by the editors of *Building Design and Construction*, half of the developers of multifamily housing use in-house designers for all or

14. Thomas M. Stanback, Jr., et al., *Services: The New Economy*, introduction, table 1.2. Also, Harry Greenfield, *Manpower and the Growth of Producer Services*, chap. 3.

15. About 60 percent of registered architects are currently AIA members. This percentage represents a substantial increase from previous periods. As recently as 1980, the percentage was between 40 and 50.

16 "Architects in Public Agencies," pp. 3-5.

most of their projects. These developers rely more on in-house designers than developers of any other building type, with the exception of motel and hotel owners. On the other hand, government agencies, school boards, hospital clients, and the developers of commercial buildings and shopping centers almost always allocate design responsibility to some outside organization, whether a private architectural firm, a designer employed by a construction company, or a firm engaged in building rather than development. In the case of government agencies, 92 percent of projects use services outside the agencies and among shopping center developers the figure is around 70 percent.[17]

Companies that employ the largest numbers of in-house architects are not in the building business, but handle construction financing and real estate investment. These are banks and insurance companies, who use their architectural staff to assist them in making investment, mortgage, and loan decisions.[18] In addition, there are clients who hire architectural firms on a retainer basis to provide general consulting services relating to problems of building and plant maintenance. This is a long-standing procedure among universities, museums, and some commercial organizations. The successive firms set up by Ralph Adams Cram played this role for Princeton University for more than two decades. The Metropolitan Museum of Art in New York City employed Arthur Rosenblatt as vice-president in charge of design for many years, but now uses an outside firm to handle this function. These consultants evaluate existing facilities, develop programs for new buildings and for renovations, assist in the selection of other firms to handle individual projects, and design individual buildings.[19]

For many decades, the architects working for government and industry were denigrated as "captive architects." However, because of the growth in their number and the huge volume of building produc-

17. *Building Design and Construction*, December 1985. The tally excludes single-family houses, utility plants, roads, bridges, dams, and equipment not directly associated with buildings. The owners and developers who were surveyed included 80 diversified developers, 30 retail developers, 60 industrial companies, 30 multifamily developers, 30 hotel/motel/restaurant companies, 50 government agencies, 10 schools, and 10 hospital companies.

18. These are taken from a survey sponsored by the Architects in Industry Committee of the AIA, which contacted 1,531 companies, of which 481 responded. Of that group, 191, or approximately 40 percent, stated that they employed staff architects. Thomas M. Fabian, "Architects in Industry: Letter," p. 34. I have some difficulty with this survey. Portions of the original survey that I have seen present data that differ in some details from the statistics reported in Mr. Fabian's letter.

19. I am very grateful to Prof. Dana Cuff of the University of Southern California for alerting me to this dimension of architectural practice.

tion over which these architects have some influence, the AIA and many of the bigger state and local chapters now have standing committees concerned with the special problems of architects who work outside the private firm. Despite the increased role played by staff architects, the general attitude of industry, government, and non-profit organizations remains that it is more economical to hire specialist consultants from outside (table 3). Consultants have more experience in dealing with specific design and building problems and are familiar with alternative strategies developed by organizations facing problems similar to their client's. Furthermore, an employer does not face the burden of finding work for the professionals to do within the organization between projects. On the other hand, in-house architects may play a role in educating their bosses about the significance of architectural and building issues, and alerting them to the range of services that private offices are able to provide. They can, and frequently have, made employers aware of the valuable skills of architects, and thereby have enlarged the market for consultants. In addition, because they are often chosen by clients to represent them in negotiations, staff architects are in a position to ease the path for the private firms in the endless deliberations that make up the design and building process. This ability of in-house architects to stimulate their employers' interest in hiring architectural services is just one example of a more general phenomenon noted by economists: supplier-induced demand. It is regarded as a unique capacity of professionals and has been observed especially in medicine, where physicians are in a strong position to recommend the quantity of services patients should consume. As some economists have noted, [supplier-induced demand] "raises the issue of whether services are being supplied past the point which a well informed consumer would choose."[20] Their referent is medicine, but could it apply to architectural services, too? The answer architects would give to the question can be easily guessed. Despite the rise in demand, the profession is convinced that clients and the public need more extensive services, not less assistance and guidance. However, the changes which I describe in the next chapter dealing with the structure of demand suggest that clients might give the opposite answer.

---

20. Patrick Foley, Avner Shaked, and John Sutton, *The Economics of the Professions: An Introductory Guide to the Literature*, p. 11.

The New Structure
Of Demand

The growth of the overall demand for services has been accompanied by important shifts in the types of services architects are expected to provide. Many of these shifts threaten traditional ways of conceiving of the profession and its skills.

One feature of current demand that illustrates the shift is that clients are looking for services that had not formerly been identified as specific skills of the architect. These include maintenance cost estimates, post-occupancy evaluation, and building diagnostics, plus two subjects that have become major preoccupations of clients: interior architecture and space planning, and "facade architecture" or "imageability." The last two services, which I discuss further below, are linked to the growth of the commercial and office building markets.

By identifying these services as new, I do not mean to imply that demand for them was wholly lacking in the past, or that firms were unresponsive to providing these services. On the other hand, it has only been since the 1960s that many offices recognized these services as billable items, and organized their practices and promotional activities in order to highlight them.

The willingness of architectural firms to emphasize interior architecture makes good sense economically. The design of interior space, especially office space for high level personnel and floor space in department stores and other shops marketing consumer items, produces high fees for the practitioner. Interior space is also replaced much more frequently than the building shell and facades. It therefore offers the possibility of repeat work, which generally results in bigger profits.

The market for facade architecture is not a new development historically, but it does represent a definite break with the nineteenth century and modernist traditions which centered architectural interest on the total building product and its functionality. The current demand for architects to decorate the outside of buildings also incorporates a new twist in that clients will now turn to architects for just this service and nothing more. Clients in these situations either handle the structural and technical systems of the building by using in-house designers, or turn the job over to a contractor or another architectural firm than the one they use to "style" the building. The emphasis on appearance has something to do with the belief among clients that buildings with a distinctive or unusual appearance will excite public attention, thus attracting a large number of more affluent tenants. As the Philadelphia architect and critic Stephen Kieran points out, it is a form of consumer packaging. Architectural firms respond to the demand by promoting their special style:

> Given the competition between a relatively large number of architectural firms for a limited number of projects, the market economy has created unprecedented demand for image differentiation within the profession itself. At least at the highest levels of practice, uniqueness is a prerequisite for survival. Since the core service performed by all architects is essentially the same, differentiation must be achieved in the secondary, formal realm. Packaging, style, special optional features, brand names, and overall quality can all be manipulated to establish specific, identifiable position within the marketplace. These formal qualities can and indeed do vary a great deal in our society of plenty. Architecturally speaking, buildings are packages and styled today with uniqueness in mind. Further, certain architects become identified with special features that often appear in their work, and, just as automobiles carry the brand name of their maker, so too do many self-consciously made buildings.[1]

Because there is still strong pressure within the profession in support of the belief that an architect should assume responsibility for the total building product, few firms choose to present itself as willing to design only facades and interior ornament. In fact, however, there are several firms that are selected by clients largely for this reason, including many of the firms that have achieved recognition because of their post-modern stylistic inventions. Should clients not be familiar with the availability of this service, there are books and manuals that urge them to think in these terms. Thus the author of a guide to real estate development writes:

> It is not advisable to try to change the style of an architect; but to find an architect who in the opinion of the market analyst is in demand. The architect who is in focus with consumer demands and is flexible in his design should be the target of the developer.[2]

The interest of clients in finding architects who are prepared to confine their services to specific features of the product or particular

---

1. Stephen Kieran, "The Architecture of Plenty: Theory and Design in the Marketing Age," p. 107.
2. Gene Phillippo, *The Professional Guide to Real Estate Development*, p. 87.

stages of the building process has become a general characteristic of the new demand. This is not restricted to issues of interior decor or esthetic questions. Many jobs are limited to a feasibility study, program development, schematic layouts, or diagnosis and evaluation of problems in existing buildings. Often the performance of these services will lead to further work on the project or another job for the same client. Just as frequently, however, the scope of the assignment is confined to the original commission.

Once a firm gets a job it does not always know the tasks the project will involve. The official AIA handbooks and guides to practice warn architects to be wary of this situation, and advise writing the contract so as to guard against changes in the job description. The advice, however, is impractical. Clear and precise provisions stating the scope of service benefit the architect should the client wish later to reduce the commission, but firms prefer to leave certain arrangements ambiguous in hopes the job will expand. Unpredictability can result from the client's bureaucratic system of management. Under this management system, many levels within the hierarchy of the organization can be assigned responsibility for deciding the range of services required: in-house professionals, financial officers, and different user groups. At the chief executive level, family members and friends sometimes get into the act. The difficulties are intensified when the building problem is complex or when the project is for a relatively new building type such as many organizations are now constructing in order to capitalize on advances in building technology:

> often there is no one "client"—no single individual on the owner's side who can identify the required criteria. The information has to come from multiple sources: the plant engineer, the security supervisor, the office manager... and the accounting or data processing department. Sometimes a facilities manager may attempt to act as middleman between these departments and the architect—with varying degrees of success.[3]

With so many participants, the work that will be specified in the final commission is frequently difficult to forecast, for the client and for the architect.

The structure of demand is also changing because coordination of the design and building process is becoming the domain of other professionals. Architects believe this role is important because it is the only method which guarantees that the building will be com-

---

3. Bea Sennewald, "Smart Buildings: Facts, Myths and Implications," p. 23.

pleted as it has been designed. Centuries of experience with the
building process have demonstrated the inclination of clients and
contractors to modify the design during the construction stage. The
gradual loss of the function of coordinating all the work that goes
into the making of a building results partly from the contemporary
definition of the architect as a purveyor of specialized technical services. It is because many clients now believe that architects, and
professionals generally, are knowledgeable only in limited areas that
they have taken over the coordination function themselves, either by
employing their own staff or by hiring construction firms who have a
reputation for managing complex operations. With the loss of the in-
tegrative function, many leaders in the profession fear that *the* major
rationale for the architect to maintain extensive control over projects
has been lost. On the other hand, critics of the profession have noted
that the profession itself has collaborated in the dispersal of its
authority, believing that in this way architects can reduce their moral
and legal liability for performance failures.[4]

Anxiety arising from fear of losing control of work routines is now
found among all parties to the building process. It may simply reflect
the inherent complexity of the process and therefore the persistent
instability of the industry. With progress going on in building technology, and as a result of changing policies and resources, none of the
participating individuals and groups can be sure their influence will
continue at the same level. Even carpenters, often regarded as the
most solid and assured of all building workers, display this concern.
In his book on housebuilding, Kidder refers to a builder who "argues
that the occupation has not suffered from the new tools and techniques...He worries instead about the disappearance of such tasks as
door and window making, and the carpenter's loss of control over
building sites to architects, engineers, speculators and general contractors."[5]

Of the features changing the structure of demand, the most important remains to be mentioned. It is also the most positive change
from the point of view of the profession. This is the big expansion in
the range of building types that Americans now believe requires the
intervention of professional architects. Among the building types
that fall into this category are the ordinary commercial or spec office
building and the standard housing development and tract house. In
the past, the majority of office buildings were designed by engineers,

4. Julian E. Lange and D. Quinn Mills, *The Construction Industry: Balance Wheel of the
Economy*, p. 7.
5. Tracy Kidder, *House*, p. 135.

while the mass produced tract house was designed by developers or individual owners using stock plans.[6] The significance of this market for demand is that the tract house represents one-third of the total volume of new building constructed each year, and the office building an additional 15 percent. In view of these statistics, it is not surprising that by 1982, work on commercial buildings was the single largest source of architectural firm receipts. Forty-five percent of firm receipts were derived from commercial buildings, up from 31 percent in 1972 (table 4).[7] Fifty percent of housing units are currently designed by architects, but this does not show up prominently in the statistics of private firms. The architects who are involved are mostly staff members of housing and development firms.[8]

The use of architects for secular and commercial building types is a considerable switch from practice in the nineteenth and earlier decades of the twentieth century. According to the historian Sarah Landau,

> Churches and church-related buildings constituted the greatest proportion of architect-designed buildings erected in America during the first three-quarters of the nineteenth century, as witnessed by the huge production of Richard Upjohn's firm; and the church, considering all denominations collectively, continued to be a major patron of artistic, if not utilitarian, architecture until World War I.[9]

Factories and workers' housing associated with them were not regarded as buildings deserving the attention of architects until the last quarter of the nineteenth century. Office and other commercial buildings first entered the architectural canon at the end of the nineteenth century, with the work of the great Chicago architects Adler and Sullivan, Jenney, Root, and Burnham. Office buildings, warehouses, industrial facilities, and retail outlets accounted for two-thirds of the total number of Adler and Sullivan's commissions, with commercial construction representing the major share.[10]

6. Robert Gutman, "Architects in the Home-Building Industry," p. 210.

7. Commercial buildings also represent the largest percentage of the practice of AIA member firms polled in 1977. See Magali Sarfatti Larson, George Leon, and Jay Bolick, "The Professional Supply of Design: A Descriptive Study of Architectural Firms," table 10.9.

8. The estimate of the portion of housing units designed by architects, and the method for arriving at it, are discussed in Robert Gutman, *The Design of American Housing*, pp. 8-9.

9. Sarah B. Landau, *Edward T. and William A. Potter: American Victorian Architects*, pp. 15-16.

10. Richard Levy, *The Professionalization of American Architects and Civil Engineers, 1865-1917*, p. 45.

Modern clients, in their search for technical advice, have turned to architects for the design of many ordinary buildings (table 4). However, this phenomenon is also very much an indication of the consciousness alluded to earlier, involving recognition that architecture is an art and that art has economic value and carries social benefit. Buildings that are esthetically pleasing are admired for the pleasure they give and also because buildings so endowed are more likely to attract tenants and yield higher rents. A corporate headquarters is now a "giant architectural logo," making the company conspicuous in the urban landscape. Fashionable interior design is justified on the grounds that it contributes to employee morale and aids recruitment.[11] The chief executive of Proctor and Gamble is convinced, for example, that the luxurious interior fittings of the headquarters building designed by Kohn, Pedersen and Fox have been a big help in overcoming the resistance of managerial talent to moving to Cincinnati.[12]

The new emphasis on design quality is clear from the management and marketing policies of the big comprehensive practices. Many of them are trying to overcome a reputation for designing efficient but dull buildings by hiring architects with established reputations as designers. It tells us something about the changing market for architecture that firms should be worrying about this issue, given the fact that many other offices aspire to be known for their competence in dealing with the technical and practical problems of buildings. This new consciousness accounts, for example, for the venerable New York firm of Wank, Adams, Slavin and Associates making Susana Torre a partner in charge of design; and the Hillier Group, in Princeton, New Jersey, hiring Alan Chimacoff to be its director of design.[13] The Hillier Group ranked twentieth in business volume on the list of architectural giants compiled by *Corporate Design and Realty* for 1986, but not until it appointed Chimacoff did it begin to be short-listed in major national design competitions. A more traditional technique that is becoming more widespread is for

---

11. Environmental design researchers are more interested in the effect of room size, layout, and equipment on employee morale. These effects have been explored recently in a number of studies, many of which are described in two books: Jean D. Wineman, ed., *Behavioral Issues in Office Design* and Mary E. Dolden and Robertson Ward, Jr., *The Impact of the Work Environment on Productivity.*

12. Joseph Giovannini is the author of the phrase "giant architectural logos," which appears in his article "The Grand Reach of Corporate Architecture." The claim of the head of Proctor and Gamble is from the *Economist,* London, April 12-18, 1986, p. 97.

13. The effort to incorporate the talents and skills of independent, established designers within larger, mostly commercial practices, does not always work out. Ms. Torre resumed her own practice in 1987, in partnership with Raymond Beeler.

firms to undertake joint ventures with a celebrated designer for purposes of entering a competition, or to pursue a specific job. This strategy is in part a response to the growth of cultural and economic elites in America's smaller cities who want their public and institutional buildings to count on the national scene. As a result of this movement, cities of the middle rank, such as Atlanta, Des Moines, Syracuse, Seattle, Cincinnati, Austin, and San Diego, have been getting buildings designed by Johnson, Pei, Venturi, and Graves. All these strategies, taken together, are a sign that the profession has been following the acquisition, merger, and contractual models that are standard now throughout the industries of capitalist economies.

Another example of the changing structure of demand is seen in the measures clients take for obtaining services. Corporate and institutional clients in particular exhibit a reasonably explicit strategy in choosing firms. A standard approach is to designate classes of building types and then seek different kinds of architectural groups to handle the jobs for each class. Routine building problems are dealt with by the facilities management department or other in-house staff. Buildings for which there are many established precedents in the architectural tradition, but which the company in question has not constructed previously, are given to competent, experienced but undistinguished architectural firms. Corporate headquarters for which the company may want high visibility, or building problems that demand innovative solutions, are assigned to firms known for their record in producing highly imageable structures, or for experimental achievements in other realms of architecture. Corporate and institutional clients are able to adopt rational procedures because of their extensive experience with construction programs, and their large physical planning and building maintenance departments.

The rationality of clients' market behavior is evidence that their willingness to interview a large number of firms should not be interpreted as confusion on their part about the types of service they require. The accessibility of clients comes as a surprise to many architects of an older generation who were brought up to believe that the only way to get a job was through private, and often hidden, contacts and connections. The market is much more open now, consistent with the establishment of routine application, selection, and purchasing procedures in many areas of business and government. The readiness to interview a dozen or more offices simply indicates that clients are trying to identify the firms that are most likely to meet specific needs, or whose style of operations meshes best with the client's management and organizational style. There is a wide range of questions clients may have in mind. Does the firm have demonstrable capability for the project? Does the information presented in the firm's brochure correspond to the reality of the firm's organization and skills? What procedures does the firm adopt for making sure work will keep to schedule? Who are the individuals the clients will be dealing with in the architectural firm?

Current demand requires that architects be competent at promoting and selling their firm. Although the problem of dealing with the entrepreneurial side of practice is an old issue for the profession, some architects seem to resent the requirement more now than ever before. They are irritated by the strenuousness of the effort they have to make to get a job: finding out how they are perceived by the client community; developing and distributing different versions of a brochure; spending time soliciting clients by mail, phone, and personal visits; and getting advice from marketing specialists and public relation consultants. Architects who are disturbed by the emphasis put on these activities prefer the collective efforts to establish the importance of the profession with the public and among the community of potential clients. These efforts include programs of awards given to what architects define as good buildings or urban designs, career days sponsored by the profession in high schools, the development of materials for lessons in architecture in the elementary schools, the advocacy of landmark and preservation legislation, and television programs intended to foster the awareness of architectural values.

What architects resent most about marketing programs is the assumed implication that architecture is a business enterprise rather than a profession, and that the business side is taking precedence and guiding the definition of the field. Architects recognize that they can survive in practice only by getting jobs, managing their offices efficiently, pleasing clients, and making a profit. However, some in the profession fear the extent to which these activities, in effect, advertise the business side of their work to clients and the public. To many architects being known as a business person means that clients will imagine they place profitability and self-interest ahead of concern for building quality and the well-being of the client. The latter concerns are the hallmark of professionalism. They are what architects like to have it thought distinguish them from builders, contractors, stock plan designers, and purely commercial operators in the building industry.

I believe architects ought to worry about the heavy emphasis the AIA and many firms now place on marketing programs. It is all too consistent with the view of the profession in many sectors of the community, especially among building users and the general public. Users of buildings and urban environments are very suspicious of architects' motives. The profession is looked upon as venal and selfish. Architects are perceived as people who are mainly interested in advancing, often on the basis of spurious arguments, the economic interests of building owners and developers; and therefore, indirectly, the wealth of professionals themselves. The public's trust in the fidelity of the profession is being undermined. The importance of this trust is the large part it plays in enforcing the client's respect for architects. This respect is based only circumstantially on confidence in technical skill. More important for the continuation of respect is the belief that architects will apply their skill not only for the benefit of the persons who pay their fees but also in response to the interests of persons, groups, and communities beyond the purview of the immediate client. For this reason, one can say that the public's and the user's conviction that the architect is indeed committed to the professional ideal is a fundamental source of the demand for the services of architectural firms. Architects who ignore this fact in their selling efforts imperil the future of their own practices and the practices of other architects.

Although I believe it is important to recognize the hazards of the marketing mentality, it is unrealistic to expect offices to ignore the economic pressures impinging on all professions and producer services in this period of growing competition. Indeed, it is possible that market research makes a positive contribution to the quality of the environment by alerting architects to the services and building types for which there is a social and economic need. These marketing programs thereby enable offices to respond to the current requirements of clients, users, and the public. By allowing firms to identify the markets they wish to enter, market studies also give practitioners better control in deciding the kind of work they wish to do.

I have reviewed a half-dozen or more changes occurring in the structure of demand. These changes help us to understand why the large firms with fifty or more employees have become critical influences within the profession. An office that commands a wide range of skills, employs a multidisciplinary staff, and operates in many cities and countries is attractive to the big national and international clients, with diverse building and planning needs. However, I also have noted that despite the economic ascendancy of the large firms, the profession continues to be dominated numerically by offices with fewer than twenty employees. Some of the factors that make it possible for these smaller organization to survive have been discussed already, and more are dealt with in subsequent chapters. The nature of architectural work and the organization of the building process make it feasible for a small design team to handle the complex program of a much larger client organization. In addition, the smaller firms often specialize in one particular service or skill required in modern buildings. There are also many simple building projects that small firms can handle themselves. However, it would be incorrect to conclude from these facts that only the biggest firms represent a new type of practice. The way the small firms operate, too, is different from the situation of the majority of the profession in the 1950s or 1960s. Furthermore, what I call the small office includes more architects and other technical personnel than it used to: the small office is a bigger small office than it was in the recent past. A major reason for this trend, too, is the changing structure of demand for services.

The Supply of Architects and Firms

The professional architects who are principals or employees of the 25,000 firms discussed in the previous chapter are drawn from approximately 90,000 architects in the country. The 90,000 is an estimate.[1] The census figures are self-reported, and it is likely that some people who call themselves architects lack the qualifications recognized by the building community. On the other hand, several thousand men and women with professional training in architecture have shifted careers and may now identify with their new occupations. Despite these flaws, the Census enumerations, which were discounted by the AIA and other groups in the profession in the past, have been shown to be reasonably accurate.[2]

Of the estimated 90,000 architects, between 65,000 and 70,000 are principals or employees of private architectural or engineering firms. Seventy thousand of the 90,000 are *licensed* architects, that is, they have successfully completed the registration requirements of the state governments. Forty thousand of the licensed architects work for private architectural offices that have employees, with the others self-employed in one-person firms, working for engineering and surveying offices, or employed elsewhere in the building industry. From the analysis of the information about all architects and the licensed architects, it is reasonable to conclude that 15,000–20,000 are now employed outside the mainstream of traditional practice, working for government agencies, contractors, materials producers and developers, mortgage banks and other construction lenders, and builders (table 7). Relatively few architects with professional degrees work in occupations clearly unrelated to architecture.[3]

---

1. The Census Bureau reported 108,000 architects in 1985, based on its Current Population Survey. However, the occupation by industry analysis in the 1980 census indicated that about 15,000 of this number were landscape architects and 3000 were naval architects. See table 7 in this book and U.S. Department of Labor, Bureau of Labor Statistics, "The Job Outlook in Brief."

2. Turpin C. Bannister, *The Architect at Mid-Century: Evolution and Achievement*, p. 65, n. 19.

3. A survey of the experiences of graduates from professional programs that covered the classes of 1967, 1972, and 1977, found that 7–9 percent were working at jobs clearly unrelated to architecture. The 1977 survey was conducted by the Association of the Collegiate Schools of Architecture. See Roger Schluntz, "Alternative Careers of Architectural Graduates."

The explosion in the numbers in the profession began soon after the end of the Second World War (table 5). The most dramatic measure of the growth is the ratio of architects to the number of people living in urban areas (table 6). Between 1850, when the Bureau of the Census first began to collect occupational information, and 1920, the ratio of architects to the number of people living in urban areas doubled. There was actually a decline in the ratio over the next four decades, but then after 1960 the ratio started to go up. There are over five architects to every 10,000 urban residents, the highest level in American history, more than three times the ratio of 1850, and twice that of 1960 (table 6 and chart 1). Actually the big jump in the number of architects has occurred very recently, in the ten years between 1970 and 1980. There were only 56,000 architects in the nation in 1970. The major increase in terms of percentage growth took place between 1960 and 1980. Over the course of this twenty year period the number of architects tripled, from 30,000 to the present number.[4]

The rapid growth in the number of architects over the last twenty years is astounding. Architecture has become the fastest growing of all the major professions, far outstripping the increases even of lawyers (table 6). The number is especially remarkable when one considers that there were more architects in the United States by 1984 than the Bureau of Labor Statistics predicted would exist by 1990.[5]

The rate of increase in the number of architects has far exceeded the growth rate in the number of firms. For example, during the decade of the 1970s, when the number of architects increased by approximately 60 percent, the number of private architectural firms increased by only 20 percent. The difference between the two rates reflects the growth in firm size.

Recent employment statistics indicate that 98 percent of architects are working. This figure has remained more or less constant since the end of World War II, except for the mid–1970s, when architectural employment declined by 12 percent, because of the rise in construction costs and general high inflation following the first "oil shock."[6] Low unemployment rates have been a feature of the profession over the last forty years because downturns in construction are

---

4 .Most of these data are taken from Robert Gutman and Barbara Westergaard, "Architecture among the Professions," a report prepared for the Architectural Education Study, 1974, and subsequent revisions.

5. Max L. Carey, "Occupational Employment Growth through 1990," p. 49, table 2.

6. Judith Blau, *Architects and Firms*, p. 115-17.

often limited to particular regions of the country. For example, when jobs in New York in 1976 diminished because of that city's financial crisis, building was still expanding in the South, Southwest, and Far West. Similarly, when the Midwest and the Northeast were hit by the inflation in construction costs following the oil embargoes of the 1970s, the economies of the oil-producing states were expanding. More recently architects have found it necessary to leave the Southwest to find work in the Far West and the Northeast. Fortunately for architects, the profession socializes them to itinerant careers, so they seem to accept the necessity of these moves better than members of many other occupations.

Another important contributor to high employment rates is the growth in job opportunities for architects outside the conventional forms of practice. I said that 15,000–20,000 architects now fall into this category. Major areas of job growth are in retail trade and the finance, insurance, and real estate industries (table 7). Well-designed, eye-catching facilities are regarded as important in stimulating department store sales. Architects' skill at producing rentable space has proven useful to real estate developers and lending institutions. In addition, there is demand for several new types of design services, including exhibition development, product development, film production, graphics packaging, and computer-aided design systems. Architects have become active in all these areas. They also have been getting work in the offices of landscape architects and interior designers, a very recent development that reverses the standard and still dominant direction of the relationship between architecture and these two professions.

Despite high employment rates and evidence of expanding demand, leaders in the profession and some educators continue to express concern about the possible surplus of architects and architectural firms. At the beginning of "The Rising Demand for Architectural Services," I discussed some of the reasons for the widespread pessimism and anxiety, but there are other factors at work as well. A very important reason is that architecture has a history of vulnerability to economic fluctuations. In the nineteenth and the first half of the twentieth century high rates of employment were followed regularly by periods of unemployment. In 1898, when college education was first being established as the proper path for entering the profession, Columbia University reported that of the 650 students granted architecture degrees during the period 1881-1898, only 120 had found work in the field. A survey conducted of U.S. architects during the Great Depression estimated that *90 percent* were idle.[7] In Great Britain during the early 1930s, the Architectural Association in London was able to place only half the number of graduates that it could in normal times.[8] This information, combined with the more favorable situation since World War II, suggests a trend toward increasing stability in architectural employment. The trend is probably tied to the growth of the big, comprehensive firms as well as the direct employment of architects by clients and organizations of the building industry.[9]

The development of the large firm and the addition of so many architects to the profession could not have taken place if demand had not increased in the manner discussed in previous chapters. However, the immediate cause of the supply is the tremendous expansion in the number and size of architecture schools that has occurred since the Second World War, which made available an unprecedented number of men and women with professional training. Enrollments in professional degree programs, which totaled 4,500 in 1930, had increased to 20,000 by 1980.[10] The growth resulted partly from the increase in the number of professional programs, from forty-seven in the United States in 1930, to over eighty in 1980. However, it also was the consequence of enrollment increases in existing programs. For example, the forty-seven programs that had 4,500 students in 1930 enrolled 14,000 students by 1970 (table 8 and chart 2).[11] The enrollment expansion also shows up in the number of degrees awarded. Between 1971 and 1983, the number of bachelor's degrees awarded annually in architecture grew from 5,500 to 9,800. Only about one-third of these were so-called first professional degrees, i.e., degrees awarded by

7. For the Columbia estimates, see Levy, *Professionalization*, p. 131. The situation during the Great Depression is described in Bonnie F. Schwartz, *The Civil Works Administration, 1933–1934*, p. 130.

8. Walter M. Kotschnig, *Unemployment in the Learned Professions*, p. 123.

9. Architecture has long been thought to be a profession with relatively high attrition rates. The data are not clear on this matter, but if it has been so, the rise in the demand for services is probably leading to more graduates staying in the profession and going on to be licensed. For a discussion of earlier rates of attrition see Robert Gutman and Barbara Westergaard, "What Architecture Schools Know about Their Graduates."

10. These numbers refer to the sum of enrolled students in bachelor's and master's degree programs accredited by the National Architectural Accrediting Board. If other programs offering training in architecture are included, the 1980 number is probably closer to 25,000.

11. The information about enrollments in the 47 schools is reported in an unpublished paper prepared for the Architectural Education Study, 1974. Vasco Fernandez, Robert Gutman, and Barbara Westergaard, "Enrollment Trends in Schools of Architecture, 1930–1972."

programs that are accredited by the NAAB and recognized by the state boards that license architects. Master's degrees, almost all of which were professional degrees, doubled over the same period. Fifteen hundred masters degrees were awarded by NAAB-accredited schools in 1985. They were equally divided between first and second professional degrees. In other words, approximately 4,000 newly qualified students with first professional degrees have been entering the labor market annually in recent years. In addition, many of the 6,000 students who graduate from four-year colleges each year without professional degrees, but who have nevertheless had substantial training in architecture, are also getting jobs in the field.[12]

The reasons for the tremendous rate of expansion in the supply of architects are not all that clear. It is hard to believe that young people come into the schools because they are attracted by the pay levels in the profession. Of course, it may be that students are not aware of how poorly paid architects are compared to other professionals of equivalent prestige and status. As a profession, architecture is confusing, as the sociologist John Cullen has pointed out. For most professions, there is a clustering of positive attributes, so that a profession that ranks high in prestige also pays better than other professions. This rule applies in law and medicine but not in architecture.[13] It is more probable that the field is appealing because there are few other professions for which one can qualify with only five years of higher education. Also architecture is regarded as a profession in which there are good opportunities for self-expression and individual creativity. And compared to other fields endowed with this image, such as studio art, it offers relative job security. This is surely a factor among candidates who enter the three-year professional degree programs at the master's level. A very large percentage of the

12. The data on recent enrollment and degrees awarded from 1973 onward are taken from three sources: U.S. Department of Commerce, Bureau of the Census, *Statistical Abstract of the United States, 1986*, p. 159; U.S. Office, then Department, of Education, *Digest of Educational Statistics*, annually beginning with 1964–65; and the annual statistical reports of the National Architectural Accrediting Board. The numbers reported by the government sources are generally higher than the NAAB data, although the trends of both types of data are consistent with each other. The difference reflects the fact that not all programs offering instruction in architecture are recognized by the NAAB.

13. The clustering pattern that Cullen identifies extends to other attributes of professions, including the duration of the training period and the percentage of professionals who are self-employed. John Cullen, "Structural Aspects of the Architectural Profession."

students in these programs majored as undergraduates in painting, sculpture, graphics, fashion, and art history.[14]

In my judgment, the huge supply of architects is having other effects that in some respects are more damaging to the morale of the profession over the long-run than the hazards of possible future high unemployment. One such danger is that too many qualified architects are working at levels below their talent and training. This is particularly characteristic of recent cohorts entering the job market. Many young architects do routine drafting jobs that just a few decades ago were done by technicians or men and women with two-year degrees from vocational and trade schools. The experience graduates are getting in these jobs is an essential part of their apprenticeship, and compensates for the limitations of the training provided by the schools in this period of increasing academization of professional education. However, the distressing feature of the current system is that many architects with professional degrees may remain locked in relatively routine, menial, and low-paying jobs for most of their career (table 9).

The downgrading of the work responsibilities of individuals with professional degrees is a major concern in many professions, including medicine, the profession with the most powerful position in the marketplace. Apparently a large number of physicians who have been licensed as specialists are forced, because of the lack of suitable openings, to practice family medicine. From the point of view of the patient, this trend can be considered beneficial. It may be that the availability of better-trained architects at low-level positions also is an advantage to firms and to clients. However, looked at from the perspective of the profession as a whole, both in medicine and in architecture, the overtrained individual can represent a waste of resources. The use of overtrained professionals also drives up the cost of care or service. Partly because of concern over these developments, the AMA has been calling the attention of the public to a prospective oversupply of physicians, and advocating that medical school admissions be reduced. The architectural profession is worried about too many architects, but there has been very little attention to the plight of the younger professionals who may be overeducated for tasks they are expected to perform in the office.

14. A large percentage of the students entering the three-year first professional degree programs are women. In some schools women make up over 50 percent of the entering class. The large number of women applying to schools of architecture is currently an important factor in their continued high enrollments. To this extent, architectural education in the United States is following a pattern well established since the Second World War in some of the Latin countries of Europe.

A second effect of the larger number of architects is the growth in competition within the profession. Greater competitiveness, which I say more about below, is having certain positive consequences in forcing architects to explore new approaches to practice; and this new resourcefulness benefits clients. However, increased competition is also placing greater burdens on the operations of firms and the conduct of a career, and for these reasons may be undermining the professional standards of the field.

The large labor supply also results in reducing the pay and income of architects. This works in two ways. The large number of firms bidding for jobs makes it more difficult to raise fees to a level that would make practice more profitable. Also, the abundant supply of men and women with professional degrees induces them to sell their labor power and skill more cheaply than if fewer architects were competing for jobs. It is a sign that architecture is a profession and not just a business that many local chapters as well as the national AIA have been engaged in efforts to raise the compensation level of employees. The typical enterprise in a non-professional field would probably ignore this problem, and reap the benefits of a large, relatively inexpensive supply of labor.

Most of these difficulties are likely to become more serious over the coming decade if there is no reduction in the volume of students graduating with professional degrees. The schools have resisted the effort to consider the question, using as their rationale the fact that applications to the schools have continued to hold up well. However, the continued high level of applications is not by itself a basis for making judgments about the problems facing the profession that stem from the supply of architects. The professional community is disposed to consider the problem, but lacks influence because in the American system of professional education, the schools are relatively independent. The policies of the schools are developed in response to university administrations, which are only minimally affected by the opinions of the professional associations.[15] I believe it is welcome news, therefore, that discussion has been started about limiting enrollment in the schools. For example, for the session it conducted at the spring 1987 meeting of the Association of Collegiate Schools of Architecture, the Architects in Education Committee of the AIA issued a call for papers that would address these questions, among others: Are there too many students of architecture? Will there be too many architects? How does one determine what is "too many"? There is also increasing discussion in the

15. Robert Gutman, "Education and the World of Practice."

profession's trade press of the problems of education, including the large enrollments; and venerable organizations, such as the National Institute of Architectural Education, are beginning to press the schools and the profession to consider the relations between education and practice. During the 1930s, when the volume of construction work went down precipitously, applications and architectural enrollments dwindled, too. The process was the result of market decisions by prospective students and had no connection to a policy advocated by the AIA or the ACSA. If a long-run decline in construction volume were to occur once more, obviously something like the enrollment decline of the 1930s would be repeated. However, it is again likely to result from market decisions by groups of individuals rather than from policy decisions by the profession.[16]

16. Fernandez, Gutman, and Westergaard, "Enrollment Trends."

Bigger and More
Complex Buildings

One and one half million new buildings have been constructed annually in the United States during the 1980s. About 900,000 of these structures are housing, the majority single-family residences. The remaining 600,000 buildings have served a range of commercial, institutional, and public functions. There have also been 750,000 building renovations in the typical year during the decade.[1] It is very likely that recent additions to the building stock are on the average larger in square footage, bulk and ground coverage than projects of previous eras.

The emergence of the large scale and complex building is setting the standard for the skills architects must present to clients and the manner in which they organize and present these skills as a means of constituting a practice. These projects establish a norm even though only 43 percent of the American non-residential building inventory encloses over 5,000 square feet, only 5 percent of our building stock is made up of structures containing more than 50,000 square feet, and only 2 percent contains over 100,000 square feet. (Obviously the size of the average building would be reduced if housing were included in these data.) A major reason why the small percentage of the stock represented by buildings of over 50,000 and 100,000 square feet can be such an influential model for practice is that these two categories contain almost one-half and one-third respectively of the nation's non-residential space.[2] The non-residential buildings, which include commercial projects, public facilities, and institutional and industrial buildings, are the source of 75 percent of the work of the 12,000 architectural firms that have one or more employees. For the biggest firms with larger staffs, the percentage is even higher.[3] These facts reinforce the conclusion stated ear-

1. These estimates have been prepared from data published in several successive issues of the *Construction Review*, a publication of the U.S. Department of Commerce and the Bureau of the Census. A fuller analysis of the data from which the estimates are derived is contained in an appendix to my paper, "Patrons in Spite of Themselves." The appendix is available from the author.
2. The data about the distribution of building space are reported in an account of the research being conducted by Prof. Francis Ventre. See *Environmental Design Research News*, 17, no. 3 (May–June 1986), p. 7. A fuller discussion of some of Ventre's analysis is included in his article "Myth and Paradox in the Building Enterprise."
3. Gutman, Westergaard and Hicks, "The Structure of Design Firms," tables 23 and 27.

lier that a significant portion of architects in the United States are still engaged in designing small buildings and houses.

These relations between the scale of building production and architectural practice are illustrated by the twenty buildings that won national honor awards from the AIA in 1987. Eight were houses and twelve were non-residential buildings. Of the twelve non-residential buildings, six, or one-half, contained over 50,000 square feet. Of the six, five enclosed 100,000 square feet or more. The six buildings were Graves's Humana headquarters; the Proctor and Gamble headquarters, in Cincinnati, by Kohn, Pedersen and Fox; the Ravenswood Regional Library by Hammond, Beeby and Babka; Murphy-Jahn's O'Hare Rapid Transit Station; the SOM National Commercial Bank in Saudi Arabia; and the Lewis Thomas Molecular Biology Building at Princeton by Venturi, Rauch and Scott-Brown. [4]

The size characteristics of the buildings constructed recently derive in part from the escalating value of land, which makes it economically profitable to construct buildings on certain urban sites only if every dollar of real estate value can be squeezed into and over them. The technological feasibility of tall buildings is, in turn, a major factor behind the rise in land values. New technologies and materials that make it possible to construct tall structures or span wide distances also contribute to the bigger scale of buildings of other types. So do the space requirements of large organizations, including universities, research and development companies, and factories, that shelter a broad range of personnel and activities under one roof or among groups of smaller buildings located in a campus setting.[5]

It is important to realize, too, that the current scale of building could not have developed without huge amounts of capital that have become available for construction. A good deal of the recent growth is the result of policy decisions advocated by economic planners and the federal government on the assumption that new industrial and commercial building will help to halt the decline in productivity and lead to economic expansion.[6] Or, as the Department of Commerce puts it, "industrial construction is also important from a public policy

---

4. *Architecture*, May 1987, pp. 122–87.

5. Peter Cowan, "Studies in the Growth, Change, and Ageing of Buildings."

6. Hedley Smyth, *Property Companies and the Construction Industry in Great Britain*, chap. 3.

perspective, because this type of capital formation provides the essential underpinnings for long-term growth in output, employment, productivity and international competitiveness."[7]

The increased scale of building has been accompanied by greater complexity in plan, structure, and fabric. Not only are individual buildings being constructed that are much more intricate than any buildings of the past, but also a larger portion of the sum total of new buildings is complex. Statistical studies examining the historical development of building complexity have not been conducted. However, the trend can be inferred from the increasing number and diversity of activities included in buildings, leading to the invention of many new building types; the variation in size and design requirements of spaces and rooms; and, most important, the development of many separate technical and environmental control "systems" which must be integrated in the total design. In the average building constructed in the 1980s, for example, a larger share of the budget has gone into the various engineering systems of foundations, superstructure, HVAC, plumbing, and engineering than into roofs, walls, partitions, and finishings. The principal change contributing to the division of costs is the expenditure for mechanical systems, which currently represent 24 percent of the budget for an average building.[8] These mechanical systems include heating and ventilating systems, information technologies, furniture and equipment systems, and services that supply processed liquids and gases, and expel polluted and contaminated air. For some recently introduced building types, such as buildings for research in molecular biology, the engineering systems can represent 60–70 percent of total project cost. Given the explosion in information technologies, and the emergence of interest in the "smart building," including now the effort of the National Association of Homebuilders to promote the "smart house," the share of the construction budget allocated to mechanical systems will probably increase still further.

Building complexity and scale emerged as major trends transforming architectural design and production with the rise of industrialism in the nineteenth century, but interest in them as characteristics governing practice is more recent. To give one example, the research

7. "Industrial Construction in the United States," *Construction Review*, January–February 1986, p. 4. The recent American situation is also affected by changes in banking laws that permitted the integration of housing capital markets with general capital markets. These historic developments are discussed in Anthony Downs, *The Revolution in Real Estate Finance.*

8. Herbert Swinburne, *Design Cost Analysis*, pp. 50–55.

laboratory developed as a building type during the nineteenth century, but buildings did not begin to be designed specifically for this use until the 1920s. Only during the 1950s did books and manuals begin to be published to assist architects in dealing with the problems of laboratory design.[9] The concept of a building as a "third environment" is a still more recent formulation. According to Fitch, the author of the concept, architecture can be thought of as "an instrument whose central function is to intervene in man's favor. The building—and, by extension, the city—has the function of lightening the stress of life; of taking the raw environmental load off man's shoulders; or permitting *homo fabricans* to focus his energies upon productive work."[10] The concept has been useful in the programming of virtually every contemporary building type, from homes and offices to factory, research, and laboratory buildings.

Another example from building history that testifies to the influence of complexity on architectural practice is the changed relation of the civil engineering profession to building design. It was not until the first decade of this century that the design of the structural systems of skyscraper office buildings involved consultation with engineers. Before then, structural design was handled by architects themselves, or by manufacturers. The relation was reciprocal: civil engineers until the early twentieth century rarely consulted architects on the esthetics of a design.[11] From the perspective of contemporary practice, it is hard to imagine that only a century ago buildings were designed on this basis. However, the average structure was smaller then, and the technology required to construct it was much simpler.

Greater scale and complexity also increase the need to involve a wider range of new disciplines and professions in project design. The reason for this is that the aspects of the building that architects are qualified to design represents *an ever smaller proportion of the total project*. According to the AIA itself, as many as twenty-five different specialist fields now exist, whose practitioners architectural firms must be ready to consult and hire. They include such specialties as acoustics; elevator design; fire protection; landscaping; lighting; mechanical, electrical, and civil engineering; soils engineering; be-

9. See Nuffield Foundation, Division for Architectural Studies, *The Design of Research Laboratories*.

10. James M. Fitch, "The Aesthetics of Function," p. 9.

11. Levy, *Professionalization*, p. 90.

havioral studies; cost estimating; energy conservation; traffic; and real estate.[12]

It is not surprising, given the degree to which complexity transfers control of building projects to other professions, that architects should continue to try limiting and managing the trend. One way they have done so over the past century, and with a sudden vehemence again recently, is to make technology into a subject for esthetic manipulation, as in the designs of the British architects, Norman Foster and Richard Rogers. The translation of social and technical ideas into principles of form is the usual method architecture uses to respond to developments in allied disciplines that have an impact on buildings and the building process. In this case, as in the typical instance from architectural history, the strategy does not really increase the architect's hold over the building process, which has been more or less permanently lost to the other building professions. However, it does improve the morale of the profession: expressing technological ideas through symbols and images makes architectural activity *appear* relevant. As a method it also helps architects deal with clients who, as Banham said about the clients for Louis Kahn's Richards Laboratories, "must wonder how it can be that a man so thoroughly out of sympathy with more than half the capital investment of a building of this kind should be entrusted with its design."[13] Banham is referring to Kahn's famous statement that he hated pipes and ductwork so thoroughly that he designed the form of the building around them, thus generating the majestic brick and concrete towers and studios that made Richards into a landmark building in the history of postwar American architecture.

The prominence of large scale and complex buildings has affected, at least in part, other aspects of building practice. For example, the number of white-collar and blue-collar workers required to program, design, and construct the average building project keeps growing. Architectural firms, therefore, must increase the amount of time they grapple with issues of managing these personnel, including hiring specialized staff to oversee their work. The number of individuals and work groups who are needed in order to produce a building these days helps to explain why architects are less directly involved in the construction side of building, and why the management of the site is now turned over to individuals and companies that are specialists in this area. According to an anthropological study of a

12. American Institute of Architects, *Architect's Handbook of Professional Practice,* chap. 10, "International Agreements."
13. Reyner Banham, *The Architecture of the Well-Tempered Environment,* p. 249.

recent project, in the construction of a 400,000-square-foot state university library, which at one point involved 250 workers on the site, no architect ever appeared. The supervisory functions were exercised by a project manager employed by the contractor, and two engineers representing the client.[14]

Because the design of many modern building types requires knowledge of a broad range of special topics outside the realm of architecture and involves a variety of participating professionals, it has been argued that the control of projects should be delegated by the owner to a construction manager.[15] This view is common among many real estate developers, corporations, large non-profit institutions, and government agencies, who feel more confident a project will be completed on time and according to budget if the total project is managed or supervised by someone other than an architect. In response to this competition, some architectural firms operating nationwide and internationally have organized construction management subsidiaries.

The proliferation of consultants required to bring a complex project to the final design stage presents the profession with a number of unresolved questions about organization, and also about the terms in which it should identify itself to the public. Should the architectural firm attempt to employ specialists on its own staff? Can it assume that the appropriate consultant will be available when needed? Do consultants have a big enough market so that they can think of reversing the relationship, employing the architects on *their* staffs? Ought architectural firms to emphasize their artistic role or their service function? Modern offices differ greatly in the responses they make to these questions. The strategy depends very much on such factors as the density of consultants and competing architectural offices in the community in which they practice, technical difficulties presented by the building types they work on, the size of their staff and their ability to turn a profit, as well as personal preferences of the principals regarding the kind of architectural work they like to be involved in, or which they wish to be known for. For example, architectural firms in New York and other large metropolitan cities almost always use consulting firms for their technical problems because so many competent specialists are available,

14. Herbert Applebaum, *Royal Blue: The Culture of Construction Workers*, p. 16.

15. The general contractor emerged in the United States in the early 1900s, and effectively eliminated "any common association between architects and tradesmen." Levy, *Professionalization*, p. 85. Thomas Cubitt was the first general contractor in Great Britain and set up his firm shortly after 1815. Frank Jenkins, *Architect and Patron*, p. 200. The construction manager seems to have been an invention of the 1930s.

and the big supply makes their fees competitive. On the other hand, almost all firms engaged in design work for housing developers, regardless of their location, use in–house staff for engineering work because the structural problems of this building type are so simple. Most offices whose status in the profession depends upon their reputation for design excellence eschew the model of comprehensive practice. They worry that they will be spread too thin.

Official AIA policy about the type of practices architects should strive to support is very clear, and has been for seventy years or more: firms must offer comprehensive services. The movement to foster this view of practice developed during World War I, when leaders of the profession realized that it no longer served their interest to emphasize the artistic role of the architect. To advocate the idea had been beneficial during the second half of the nineteenth century when architects were trying to distinguish their skills from those of builders and contractors. But with state legislatures reluctant to license people who claimed to be artists and with major construction jobs about to get underway in war industries, it became more expedient to claim that architects were able to deal with projects involving planning and technical issues and were trained to coordinate the work of other specialists. In his presidential address to the AIA convention in 1914, R. Clipson Sturgis advocated this view:

> Architecture is not an art only; it is also a science and an industry. It requires a diversity of gifts…Architects who emphasize one of these capabilities are incompletely equipped and render imperfect service as architects. The man who can perform all the services rightly demanded of an architect, and does it all well, does not exist. Architecture must be a composite work.[16]

The movement lapsed somewhat during the 1920s when, because of the relative prosperity, almost any version of a practice could achieve success. But during the Depression, with so many architects out of work, the search resumed for a professional strategy to broaden the market and challenge other building industry personnel who were matching the services of architects at much lower fees. It was his role in lending intellectual and theoretical respectability to the idea of comprehensive practice that made the coming of Walter

16. American Institute of Architects, *Proceedings of the Forty–Eighth Annual Convention*, December 2–4, 1914.

Gropius to Harvard in 1937 so important for the future of the profession. The Harvard studios were intended to simulate the building team experience for architects while they were still being trained. The hope was that graduates would appreciate the potential contribution of the multidisciplinary approach and would have learned how to manage it by the time they were ready to enter practice.[17] In the period after World War II, "extended" or comprehensive practice became well institutionalized. The idea was repeated year after year in the convention addresses delivered by AIA presidents. R. Bruce Patty, AIA president in 1985, proclaimed that: "The architect is more of a generalist. Related professionals are the specialists. Most fre-

Figure 3. Partners and associates of The Architects Collaborative at their office in Cambridge, MA, in 1953. Left to right around the table, they are: Sarah Harkness, Louis McMillan, Robert McMillan, John Harkness, Norman Fletcher, Jean Fletcher, Benjamin Thompson, Chester Nagel, and Walter Gropius.

quently it is the job of the architect to bring together all the disciplines."[18]

Given that this is the official view, it is all the more striking that so many offices are wary of it. Indeed, architects whose buildings capture the headlines, whose work is exhibited in museums, and who are the center of attention in the architectural press and in the schools of architecture are generalists in one sense, but in another sense, they violate this model repeatedly. The offices of Michael Graves and Robert A.M. Stern design a wide range of building types,

17. For statements of Gropius's ideas about the necessity of developing a comprehensive approach, see Walter Gropius, *The Scope of Total Architecture*. For a critical view of the effects of this definition of architecture on the quality of buildings, see Klaus Herdeg, *The Decorated Diagram*.

18. "Architects Are Gearing up for Technological Literacy," *ENR*, March 21, 1985, p. 46.

but the work completed in their offices is frequently limited to specialized services in design. Working drawings and specifications for
commercial and mixed use buildings designed in their offices have
been prepared by practices with which they associate. They also
have allowed construction supervision to be performed by the client,
the allied architectural firm, or a construction manager. Of course,
without their willingness to accept the new view of their function in
the building process, many of the architects named would not obtain
commissions from developers. Major sponsors, which include
developers such as Gerald Hines and Trammell Crow, educational institutions such as the University of California and the New York State
system, and corporations like Humana, can state their needs with
precision and command the authority to insist that their requirements be met. The expense involved in correcting errors of design is
enormous. Sponsors who are sympathetic to the ambitions of artist–
architects cannot afford to erect these buildings unless the designer
agrees to collaborate with a firm or a sponsor–representative who is
an expert in the problems of these facilities.

Architects have been rightly ambivalent about the consequences of
equating architecture with the esthetic aspects of design. On the one
hand, they have feared that this emphasis would undermine their
credibility and limit the demand for their services. On the other
hand, they have argued that in an increasingly competitive design
service market, this is the distinctive skill that secures their position
in competition with engineers, contractors, and less imaginative,
more routine architectural practices. This argument is, for example,
responsible for the strategy being pursued by the office in which
Robert Venturi is principal partner. The office accepts a role that
limits its participation on some, but not all, projects to the design of
the facade and non–technical spaces. It has won commissions for
major biology research buildings at Princeton, U.C.L.A., and the
University of Pennsylvania by collaborating with Payette Associates,
a Boston firm specializing in the design of research and hospital
facilities. The clients in these projects know just what they are getting, and what each architect has contributed. Thus in a report on
the Lewis Thomas Laboratories at Princeton, the first of the three
buildings completed, the legend beneath a photograph of the dedication ceremonies read as follows: "On the platform are Robert Venturi
'47, architect for the exterior of the building; [and] Thomas Payette,

Figure 4. This was Louis I. Kahn's first independent office at 1728 Spruce Street, Philadelphia, in 1948. The office was shared with a group of engineers, who are shown behind Kahn and Anne Tyng.

architect for the interior."[19]The marketing success of this approach confirms our distance from the world of the 1950s when architects like Eero Saarinen and Louis Kahn were struggling, largely with their own intellectual and organizational resources, to handle the special service and duct requirements of the General Motors Technical Center and the Richards Laboratories.

There are many explanations for the willingness of architectural firms to collaborate with offices of a different stripe or accept control by clients and developers. For example, in terms of the theory of architecture, it has become easier for architects to accommodate themselves to a more confined role because of the spread of the modernist doctrine in the arts which argues that the esthetic dimension is autonomous. Architecture resisted this doctrine longer than the other arts, because architecture, unlike painting or literature, seemed to have a connection to building function and use which was impossible to sever. However, contemporary efficiencies in the system of building production and construction technology as well as a system of practice in which sponsors or other firms are available to relieve the artist-architect from the burden of dealing with technical issues, has now liberated architects along with other artists.

If the building industry had not acquired the capacity to produce components in any shape and almost any color cheaply and quickly and if it had not developed organizations to oversee their production and installation, it is unlikely that the recent revolution toward the post–modern architectural style could have been realized. The will-

19. Princeton University, *Campaign Bulletin*, 5, no. 3 (May 1986), p. 1. It has not been sufficiently emphasized that one of Venturi's original justifications for the decorated shed approach is that it was a less expensive way of buying architecture. See *Progressive Architecture*, 51 (January 1970), p. 79.

ingness of architects to accept a task limited to esthetic arbitration fits with the preference of many clients for an architect who will confine his or her role to the esthetic or formal aspects of the project; this gives the client more latitude in dealing with pragmatic issues. The sentiment is reciprocated, in the sense that many architects believe the design impulse flourishes when it is not circumscribed by too close collaboration with consultants and industry specialists who are mostly concerned with technological and pragmatic problems. There is a fantasy element in this approach, however, since once the design leaves the architect's hands, the client or contractor is better situated to introduce modifications that are potentially disruptive to the overall design conception than if the architect selects the consultants or handles the whole job in his or her own office. The advancing importance of building complexity and mechanical systems, exemplified in the emergence of "smart buildings," increases this danger many times over.

It is precisely these hazards to control of the building task that leads critics such as Kenneth Frampton to regard the split between

Figure 5. Dedication ceremonies of Lewis Thomas Laboratory on the Princeton University Campus, 1986. The building was designed as a collaborative venture of Venturi, Rauch and Scott-Brown of Philadelphia and Payette Associates of Boston. Shown left to right on the platform in front of the building are Robert Venturi, Frederick Borsch (chaplain of the university), Laurence Rockefeller (the principal donor), Lewis Thomas (the medical scientist for whom the building is named), William Bowen (the president of Princeton), and Arnold Levine (chairman of the department of molecular biology). Thomas Payette, the other architect for the building, is hidden behind the rostrum.

design and technology not as a liberating influence, but on the contrary, as a mode of practice that makes the profession more dependent.

> Modern building is now so universally conditioned by optimized technology…that any intervention tends to be reduced either to the manipulation of elements predetermined by the imperatives of production, or to a kind of superficial masking which modern development requires for the facilitation of marketing and the maintenance of social control. Today the practice of architecture seems to be increasingly polarized between, on the one hand, a so-called "high-tech" approach predicated exclusively upon production and, on the other, the provision of a "compensatory facade" to cover the harsh realities of this universal system.[20]

Regardless of which factors account for revisions in architectural practice, the increased scale and complexity of projects have clearly had a major impact on how the profession defines its role in the building process, and therefore, on the kind of work people trained as architects do. A certain admiration has emerged in contemporary society for small-scale buildings that goes along with the growing preference for the reduced scale of houses, businesses, and communities. Nevertheless, when smaller individual buildings are constructed, they are often elements in large-scale ventures, as is the case in housing developments, shopping centers, office parks, and urban renovation schemes. Joining this trend to the fact that large and complex individual buildings are still a necessity for many economic and social functions, it is reasonable to suppose that architects in coming decades will be called upon to adapt to greater, rather than less, complexity. The types of practice that have been developing progressively since the onset of industrialization are, therefore, almost certainly the wave of the future, too. Some firms will continue to be more specialized and others will become more comprehensive. But all architects will have to learn to share responsibility with other professions and organizations of the building industry.

---

20. Kenneth Frampton, "Toward a Critical Regionalism: Six Points for an Architecture of Resistance," p. 17.

The Construction Industry

I said earlier that the growing market for architectural services is in many ways comparable to that for other producer service businesses. Although the service business perspective is an appropriate approach for examining architectural practice, it is important to recognize that architecture has a special relationship to one manufacturing industry in particular, construction. It is through this industry that architects' ideas of buildings are realized. The demand for architectural services is closely linked to the economic fortunes of construction.

The construction industry is peculiar among the industries that are significant in modern economies. Compared to other manufacturing industries that are major contributors to total GNP, it contains a large number of firms, the firms are small, businesses produce for local markets, they exhibit a high failure rate, and production is labor intensive. The similarity between these characteristics and the structure of architectural practice is striking. Architecture also contains a large percentage of small firms, offices tend to serve clients within their region, firms exhibit a high rate of economic failure, and they also use a high proportion of labor in relation to output. Architectural practice is trying to move away from these conditions by organizing larger practices, finding new sources of capital,[1] using cheaper labor power, and doing work in many areas of the nation and overseas. The construction industry is exploring similar directions. In 1982, 66 percent of general building contractors and operative builders had between one and four employees, while only 7 percent had over twenty employees.[2] Although this pattern still predominates, the industry has been undergoing dramatic changes, fueled by the need to achieve the capacity to build large, complex projects of the sort discussed above. A small number of construction firms now do a large share of the total business of the industry, while a large number of firms do a small portion of the business. This pattern, too, duplicates the situation in architectural practice. Using

1. Architectural firms in search of capital organize real estate development subsidiaries, allow themselves to become subsidiaries of companies engaged in other business, or sell shares in the public capital markets. The design firms that follow the third route are usually firms that provide services for a wide range of building types, including engineered structures. "Analysts Probe Design Firms for Keys to Market Valuation," pp. 23–24.

2. U.S. Department of Commerce, Bureau of the Census, *1982 Census of Construction Industries*, U.S. Summary, table 9, p. 13.

1982 data again, it appears that only 1.45 percent of general contractors and operative builders had over $10,000,000 in annual receipts, but that this group collected over 57 percent of the receipts of all builders in the industry.[3] In the housing field, where the construction function is often combined with real estate development, there are now firms that operate throughout the country and build 10,000–15,000 units annually. With regard to non–residential space, ten "construction giants" which function as general contractors built more than 328 million square feet of space in 1985–86, of which 119 million was built by one large producer, Turner Construction.[4] In order to reach this level of operations, the giants do business in national and international markets and command large and relatively constant sources of capital, which they generate in the form of profits and obtain through loans from major banks and insurance companies. The giants also maintain a permanent staff of competent technical personnel, whose work is supervised by professional managers.

The emergence of large–scale building firms and the increased concentration of resources in the industry are important influences on the scope and organization of architectural practice. The trends within the construction industry have been beneficial for the offices engaged in the design of big projects. Because of the existence of these contracting firms throughout the nation and abroad, architects can be reasonably certain there will be competent contractors available who understand their plans and intentions and can be counted on to execute them accurately and on time. Comprehensive practices that have themselves adopted a modern managerial style find it easy to work with contractors who espouse a similar approach.

But the emergence of the construction giants also poses a challenge to architects. Many of the largest firms are headed or managed by engineers. The engineering profession occupies a central position in the industry because there were virtually no educational programs in construction administration as such in the United States before World War II. Civil engineers filled the void.[5] They are more knowledgeable about putting buildings together and making them work than architects, and thus can compensate for the skill deficiencies of the average designer. However, engineers are typically unsympathetic to many of the esthetic aims that dominate the thinking of architects. Conflicts often arise between the two professions when

---

3. Ibid., table 10, p. 15.
4. *Corporate Design and Realty*, 5, no. 5 (May 1986), p. 52.
5. Garold B. Oberlender, "Development of Construction Research," p. 486.

both are on the building site. The important role of the modern engineers and the well-capitalized construction companies represents a break with traditional patterns in the industry. Before World War II, the average contractor's limited financial resources and lack of post–secondary education enabled architects, with their advanced and specialized training, to be the most articulate participants in the building process. Managers of construction who have risen from the trades still exist in the industry, of course, but there are fewer of them and they are becoming especially rare in the big building firms.[6]

I have already mentioned that contractors also compete with architects by taking over roles that architectural firms still regard as *their* responsibility. As the concept of construction management becomes increasingly popular, contracting firms more frequently operate as managers of the total construction process. They, rather than the architects, act on behalf of the owner, and also oversee the design. David Maister, a prominent consultant to many producer services businesses, including architects, notes that

> increasingly, through their own actions, architects are running the risk of being treated as design subcontractors. Rather than being the spouse, many architects are becoming like the household chef, respected for technical and artistic talents, but nevertheless part of the downstairs kitchen staff and paid accordingly.[7]

Construction companies also act as developers. This is standard in the field of mass housing, in which the two roles are indistinguishable. Contractors, even when they do not advertise themselves as construction managers, often do assume the design function, using in–house staff or private firms with whom they have a standard fee arrangement. These arrangements, called package deals, are very common for the construction of factories and office buildings. The British, whose survey data on this aspect of architectural and building practice appear to be more reliable than U.S. material, have reported that one–third of all factories and one–quarter of all office buildings in their country were designed under this arrangement.[8]

6. Abraham Warszawski, "Formal Education in Construction Management," p. 252.

7. David H. Maister, "Lessons in Client–Loving," p. 49. Construction firms with broad client contacts can serve as a source of referral for architects with whom they have worked successfully and whose procedures impress them.

8. Patricia M. Hillebrandt, *Economic Theory and the Construction Industry*, p. 78.

Construction/development/construction–management firms such as Morse/Diesel, CRS Sirrine, and Tishman Realty are major figures in the industry and oversee the production of tens of millions of square feet of space annually.[9] In 1986, CRS Sirrine, which was formed four years earlier through a merger of a Houston design and construction firm and a Greenville, S.C. design engineering company, ranked first in the nation in the volume of its *design* work. At that time, it had 2,700 employees, including more mechanical and electrical engineers than architects, distributed through twenty–three U.S., one South American, one African and three Asian offices.[10] These organizations often provide design capability from within their own staff. The increasing prominence of these firms, as well as other client organizations that also provide in–house design capability, was a major reason why many architectural offices were in favor of changes in the AIA code of ethics and professional conduct, to permit member firms to undertake so–called design/build practice. In this type of practice the *architectural firm* combines the roles of architect and contractor, and thus is able to provide the client with a price for the built project, in the same way the construction and construction/management firms do. The change in the ethics code was adopted on a temporary basis at the annual convention of the AIA in 1978. It became permanent in 1980. According to a study conducted for the American Institute of Architects, in 1981 13 percent of its member firms were engaged in design/build operations. The ratio is probably somewhat larger but not enormously so, at the present time.[11]

The Associated General Contractors (AGC) supported the proposal of the federal office of procurement to prevent architects from acting as construction managers on the jobs for which they were designers. The AIA resisted the proposal and it did not become official policy.[12]

Design/build has not been the panacea for architects that many firms thought it would be. As has been the case with other strategies architects have adopted to respond to changes taking place in their world, the program of involving themselves more actively in construction has produced mixed results. Design/build ventures are often unprofitable. The implementation of the desire for greater con-

9. *Corporate Design and Realty*, 5, no. 5 (May 1986).

10. *Wall Street Journal, February 2, 1982, p. 5; and "The 200 Architectural Giants of 1986," p. 40.*

11. American Institute of Architects, *Design–Build/Contracting Monitor Task Force Report.*

12. "AGC, AIA Tempers Flare over Conflict of Interest Issue," pp. 46–47.

trol over the building process brings with it some of the same agonies and anxieties that clients and contractors encounter. Especially important in this regard are the persistent management problems that arise during supervision of a building project. These difficulties, some of which are familiar to architects from running practices, are multiplied many times over in the coordination of the building trades required by a construction project. Furthermore, executives who can concentrate on construction without at the same time having responsibility for the design issues seem to be better able to accumulate the large capital resources that construction and construction–management enterprise demands. Referring to the problems of conducting a large, comprehensive design practice, Dr. Francis Duffy, a prominent British practitioner, has observed: "The paradox is that architectural firms cannot afford the activities they need to engage in, in order to survive; contractors and construction firms often can."[13]

Undertaking the twin roles of architect and developer is another widely discussed strategy for enabling architects to compete with construction firms. In this arrangement the architect becomes the owner of the land and/or buildings that the office plans and designs. He or she thus gains not only profits from professional fees, but more important, financial increments stemming from land development, project sales, and perhaps rental of the finished space. Direct participation of architects in the real estate business goes back a long time in the annals of the profession. Illustrious architects, including the Adam brothers and John Nash in England, and Charles Bullfinch and Henry H. Richardson in the United States, were developers or worked closely with them. This type of practice passed out of favor in the middle of the nineteenth century, when the leaders of the AIA and the RIBA inaugurated major programs to upgrade the image of the architect. The programs focused on shedding the commercial connection. With competition intensifying among architects, and with clients employing architects in-house, the merits of the older approach have become apparent. However, until the beginning of the 1970s, many members of the profession assumed that the code to which they had pledged support when joining the AIA, prohibited them from having an ownership interest in any project they designed.

Inhibitions inspired by fear of violating professional standards of ethics spring from misunderstandings. In an interpretation

13. Private communication to the author from Dr. Francis Duffy, principal of Duffy, Eley, Giffone and Worthington, London.

Figure 6. Drafting room in the office of Henry Hobhouse Richardson, Brookline, MA, during the early 1880s. This room, along with a library and Richardson's study, was attached to the family living quarters.

published in 1971, the AIA Board unequivocally laid this fear to rest: "As a participating owner of a project...[an architect] may perform in any role consistent with the position of ownership." As brief ethical guidelines, architects can protect their professional status—avoiding real and apparent conflicts of interest—by observing two basic rules: Inform clients and others who should know of any personal financial interest (apart from professional compensation) in the project. Contractually separate the design consultant function from the development team [presumably so that one can continue to claim a right to a professional fee].[14]

Most of the major architecture, and especially architecture/engineering firms, now participate as co–owners in some of their projects. Although the label "design/development" is not precisely applicable to these projects, one–person firms that buy an old house or two, renovate it, and then sell the newly designed, gentrified premises at a profit, are engaging in a similar kind of practice. The publicity received by John Portman Associates of Atlanta for its many successful design/development projects has provided great encouragement to the movement, particularly after Portman himself was elected to a fellowship in the AIA as a result of his accomplishments in collaboration with the Hyatt Hotel chain.[15]

14. C.W. Griffin, *Development Building: The Team Approach*, p. 6.
15. John Portman and Jonathan Barnett, *The Architect as Developer*.

However, the firms with a few employees and the medium–size firms do less design/development. Their problems of getting capital for these ventures is not unlike the difficulties of maintaining an extended line of credit for architectural operations. Indeed, it is thought that there has been a reduction in the number of offices who choose to enter the development field. According to Carol McConochie, a marketing consultant to architects,

> [architects] are finding out that being in the development business isn't the same as being in the architecture business and trying to be in both at the same time you run into mutual conflicts. You can make money in development, but only if you know what you're doing. And those who have tried to go into development with the intent of making money, but without the commitment to learning what it's all about have not done particularly well.[16]

Architects such as Richard Meier say that they run successful practices without involving themselves as developers, and, furthermore, are concerned that too much involvement with the commercial side of building and design jeopardizes architectural quality. "I don't believe that one can adequately provide professional architectural services and also be a financier or real–estate person. You're just spread too thin....It's a lame excuse to say that you have to be a financier in order to be a good architect."[17]

Meier's strictures probably represent the beliefs, certainly the aspirations, of most architects. But the commissions that Meier obtains which enable him to fulfill the professional ideal represent a minuscule percentage of the 600,000 non-residential buildings constructed each year. Probably most of the architects who have gone into design/build or design/development did not do so by choice, but rather because they felt compelled to, if their offices were to survive. So long as the construction industry assumes traditional architectural functions on its own, and continues to spawn new specialized building and design organizations, architects will also explore new approaches to practice, if only to defend their profession and its historic role.

16. Christopher K. Misner, "The A–Ds, Architect–Developers: Types and Possibilities," p. 79.
17. William Blair, "Should Architects Become Builders and Developers?" p. 10.

The Organization Client

I have referred several times to the vitality of the small office with twenty or fewer employees, which design the overwhelming majority of architectural projects. However, it is important to recall that an increasing portion of design fees have *not* been going to these firms, but instead to offices with *fifty or more employees.* The large firms dominate the profession economically. They represent the architects who deal with the big and expensive projects, the clients for which are bureaucratically managed public and private agencies and organizations. It is these clients who set the standards according to which architecture is practiced, even for small offices which have limited contacts with such clients and may rarely design buildings of the precise type these clients demand. The reason for the influence is obvious: smaller offices and younger architects aspire to provide services for the bigger clients and hope some day to win commissions for large-scale, complex buildings. In view of the central role of the big organization clients, it is necessary to understand how they view architecture. It is also important to be aware of the methods they use to deal with building questions and how they relate to architectural offices they hire.

The most significant characteristic of the organization clients is their disposition to view architectural production from a purely rational and instrumental perspective. This means that the organization clients regard buildings as capital assets, which should be managed like every other potential source of productivity, income, and profit. As a result, plans for new buildings and for the renovation of old buildings are judged in terms of their initial and maintenance costs, their resale value, their implications for corporate income, their usability as working environments and their possible effects on organizational efficiency and employee morale. All features of buildings come to be judged by these criteria, including the esthetic dimension, which traditionally was considered as outside the realm of this system of calculation.

The prevalence of the instrumental mentality in the building and design process represents the latest stage in the historical transformation of the architect-patron relationship, a process that began during the middle of the nineteenth century. It was in this period that "building committees" became the representative client for institutional projects, replacing the individual patron. The committees took over negotiations with architects, demanding that budgets be adhered to, and insisting that building regulations and health standards be observed.[1] The staffs of the organization clients have inherited the perspectives of the building committees.

The dominant position of the instrumental mentality among organization clients is indicated by the thousands of men and women in their employ working in departments with names like real estate and facilities management; building and corporate services; facilities construction; worldwide plant engineering and construction; and real estate and construction.[2] The departments vary in size, depending upon the annual construction volume of the enterprise or institution, and the degree of centralization of the planning function. They are often headed by executives with direct access to the chief officers of the corporation, but they include personnel of all ranks. For companies that lack the resources to support their own staffs to carry out these operations, trade associations can provide the requisite service with a team of roving consultants. The Building Owners and Managers Association International (BOMA), for example, offers a Building Planning Service that does this job.

> A panel of qualified experts in the construction and management of major buildings studies the objectives and drawings [of a proposed project], meets on the site, probes and questions confidentially, and for a minimum charge helps the owner and his designer make final determinations as, for example, to the effect of design on efficiency of floor layout, on floor design, on traffic, on ceiling height, lighting, economical operations, rental income, etc.[3]

To some extent, departments concerned with real estate, building and space design represent a regrouping of functions and positions that have been standard in large companies for many decades. However, the departments have been taking on new responsibilities, a trend that is encouraged by the hiring of personnel with professional degrees in different fields of design and construction. These include the established, traditional degrees in architecture and engineering; but also the occupations that are pushing for profes-

1. Jenkins, *Architect and Patron*, p. 188. I discuss some of this history in my article, "Patrons or Clients?"

2. Martin McElroy, "How Big Corporations Choose Design Firms," p. 45. The survey data from which McElroy's report is taken concentrated on the private sector, because this is the largest potential market for architects, but similar trends are occurring in non–profit and government institutions, and, of course, among real estate developers.

3. Kenneth R. Jensen, "Planning the Office Building for Ultimate Profit," in Robert Cushman and William Palmer, eds., *Businessman's Guide*, p. 137.

sional status, such as interior design; and the newest of all the relevant fields, facilities management. Facilities management is concerned primarily with evaluating and managing space in manufacturing and service facilities; although increasingly facilities managers are used by their employers to plan, design and oversee the construction of new space. The field emerged as a recognized occupation in the 1970s. It now has a professional association, the International Facility Management Association (IFMA), founded in 1980, with 1,100 members.[4] The composition of the membership reflects the interdisciplinary character of the field: architects, engineers, behavioral scientists, interior designers, and computer scientists are included. There are two journals, one American, the other British, specifically addressed to the interests of the group, and several college– and university–level departments that offer undergraduate and advanced degrees in the subject.[5] Facilities managers in corporations are reported to be in charge of some $1 *trillion* in real estate. They number many more than the membership of IFMA, perhaps 30,000 people with a professional interest in the field. Because they overlap with architects in design and supervisory roles, and at the same time often perform the functions of a client, facilities managers represent an especially unsettling and worrisome contender for the architect's authority. A further sign of the importance of the facility management market is that many of the larger architectural firms, especially those that are attempting to develop new markets for their computer installations, now advertise expertise in this area as one of their services.[6]

I have already discussed the structure of the demand for architectural services and how it has affected the methods architects are using to organize and market their skills. The staffs of organization clients are a major factor influencing the structure. With their very purposeful attitude toward building and architecture, organization clients are driving many firms to become expert on a range of techni-

4. A similar organization, the Association of Facilities Managers, was founded in the United Kingdom in 1985.

5. *The Encyclopedia of Associations*, 1986, p. 2706. The architecture and the interiors magazines have begun to acknowledge the important role facilities managers now play in commissioning design work. However, the best source of information about the various issues that concern professionals in the field themselves is *Facility Management News*, a monthly newsletter published by IFMA. The comparable British newsletter, *Facilities*, is published by the Bulstrode Press.

6. Ann Nydele, "Practice: Comes the Facilities Manager." Also "Hot New Market Lures A–E Players to Cutting Edge"; Peter S. Kimmel, "The Facility Management Market."

cal issues that architects previously ignored in practice. Clients do not necessarily expect that the technical competence will be located *within* the architectural firm. For example, in a 1985 survey by the New York chapter of the AIA of fifty corporations in the New York area, only 10 percent of the clients said they wanted a firm with in–house engineers.[7] Architectural firms, therefore, enjoy a good deal of latitude in deciding how they will respond to the clients' interests in these areas.

The instrumental view of buildings is most pronounced among business clients, including industrial and service corporations and developers, and other clients who are subject to careful budget review, such as departments and agencies of federal, state, and municipal governments. These are the clients whose entire operation is evaluated in terms of economic value. It is not surprising that they would emphasize the cost of buildings, the economic return they offer, or their impact on blue– and white–collar productivity and morale. A fact that often surprises architects when they discover it for the first time is that the instrumental view of architecture has also taken over non-profit institutions, which formerly took a more casual view of their physical plant and regarded buildings primarily as works of architectural art. This new mentality regarding buildings is especially noticeable among university and cultural organizations in the non-profit sector. With the expansion in the number of univer-sities, museums, symphony halls, and theaters, competition for fund-ing is rapidly becoming more intense. Curators, presidents, and other managers of these institutions are under increasing pressure to justify their building needs in terms similar to those that apply to the profit sector. The bigger cultural and educational institutions now employ their own in-house architects, engineers, and facilities managers, whose functions are identical with staffs in the private sec-tor.

A rational approach to construction also manifests itself in terms of how organization clients go about securing the services they need. For example, the sentimental belief that the planning for a building should begin with the appointment of an architect has begun to dis-appear. A survey in 1978 of a random sample of building owners reported that one-fifth preferred to hire the construction manager

---

7. "Survey on Architect Selection Revealed," p. 33. One reason clients may have this attitude in New York is that a great deal of so–called corporate work is really interior architecture, for which engineering competence is a very minor consideration.

before choosing an architect.[8] With the employment of in-house staffs it is common for organization clients to take projects as far as schematic design, even when they hire firms to take charge of developing the project further. This is becoming standard procedure among corporation clients and developers. As an executive of Century Corporation, the large Houston-based developer put it to an interviewer: "We've done so many large office buildings, we're able to make 90% of the decisions before the architect draws a line."[9] Building sponsors, as we have seen, are also exploring the advantages of methods for procuring building space without hiring architectural firms at all.

The domination of the architectural market by large organizations also has produced clients who are reasonably articulate and explicit in stating the criteria for evaluating buildings and the services of architects, even the procedures and methods according to which a building should be designed. A representative organization client is John Deere and Company, which has been noted for using first–rate architectural firms, including Eero Saarinen Associates and its successor firm, Roche and Dinkeloo, for some of its major projects. Its executives in charge of building operations have indicated that the company screens consultants in terms of the following written criteria:

> Nature of the project vs. consultants' expertise and previous experience in similar work;
>
> Geographic location of project vs. consultants' ability to serve;
>
> Professional standing. Excellence in design and engineering in relation to others in the profession;
>
> Availability of consultants' working staff; number of qualified people;
>
> Ability to work with and interface with Deere project staff.[10]

Comparable criteria are employed by the Public Building Service when it judges the qualifications of firms for federal government jobs. Architects have come around to the view that it is an advantage to work with clients who state their evaluation criteria explicitly. It gives firms a clearer sense of how to make their presentation, and also of whether they are likely competitors with a fair chance of win-

8. "One in Five Owners Hire CM First, Survey Shows," p. 35. However, it should be noted the same survey also reported that almost one–half the firms surveyed preferred to select the architect first.

9. "Century Development Corporation," p. 58.

10. "Deere & Company: Patron of the Architectural Arts," p. 55.

ning the commission. Also, the more accomplished offices prefer to be judged on the basis of professional qualification rather than price.

In thinking about buildings, modern organization clients make distinctions between buildings that are economical to produce but expensive to operate, or expensive to produce but economical to operate; buildings that are impressive to architects, but unsatisfactory to users, or vice versa; or buildings that will be profitable to sell but not to rent. The aim, of course, is to achieve an optimum solution in relation to diverse criteria. However, clients know that buildings serve different purposes and therefore they are willing to give some goals higher priority. IBM, for example, does not budget as much for expensive materials or architectural fees on a warehouse as it will for a regional headquarters building.

The ability of clients to distinguish between the purposes and budgets for buildings and the services required to produce them, is increasingly matched by their knowledge of the array of practices that can be hired. The pioneering research conducted by Weld Coxe and David Maister into organizational styles of the profession is also an index of the attitudes of people who purchase architectural services. Their findings divide firms into three basic types:

> *strong–idea firms*, which are organized to deliver singular expertise or innovation on unique projects. The project technology of strong–idea firms flexibly accommodates the nature of any assignment, and often depends on one or a few outstanding experts or "stars" to provide the last word.

> *strong–service firms,* which are organized to deliver experience and reliability, especially on complex assignments. Their project technology is frequently designed to provide comprehensive services to clients who want to be closely involved in the process.

> *strong–delivery firms*, which are organized to provide highly efficient service on similar or more–routine assignments, often to clients who seek more of a product than a service. The project technology of a delivery firm is designed to repeat previous solutions over and over again with highly reliable technical, cost and schedule compliance.[11]

Coxe and Maister do not identify specific firms that illustrate their typology. I would guess, however, that the offices of Frank Gehry, Michael Graves, Richard Meier, and Robert Venturi are good examples of strong–idea firms. Offices such as Ehrenkrantz and Associates or Skidmore, Owings and Merrill in New York or Geddes,

11. Weld Coxe et al., "Charting Your Course," pp. 52–53.

Brecher, Qualls and Cunningham in Philadelphia or The Architects Collaborative (TAC) in Boston fit the model of strong–service firms. The strong–delivery firms are also the more commercial firms. They have large annual billings, are not highly ranked in terms of the dominant values of the profession, and rarely, if ever, win national design awards. Commercial offices of all sizes constitute the majority of practices in the country.[12]

The sophistication of clients has been an important factor leading to increasing fragmentation and division within the profession. Because clients are now in a position to understand their own needs even before they approach an architect, and because they also have a reasonably accurate view of available services, the market for architectural firms has a discernible pattern known to both clients and architectural firms. The pattern consists of sets of identifiable niches or market segments. Each niche or segment is made up of clients with particular needs and architectural offices that attempt to serve these needs. From the perspective of the client, the aim is to discover the firms, or alternative methods of procuring services, that meet its design and building demands expeditiously. To the offices, the challenge is to identify the clients who are most likely to want to hire their services. It can be said, in other words, that fragmentation within the profession is a condition that clients help to generate and are probably interested in preserving. Architectural firms also find it to their advantage to preserve the pattern, at least once they have succeeded in understanding it and mastering its implications.

It is the task of marketing personnel and marketing consultants to provide firms with accurate information about the niches. It is also their job to help offices see themselves in relation to other sets of firms and clients, in other words, to provide them with a portrait of the overall structure of the profession. Marketing experts inside and outside the offices who grasp this pattern accurately often discourage principals and managers from making proposals on specific projects if these do not correspond to the niche the firm has chosen to occupy. It is the view of marketing professionals that an office

---

12. The Coxe–Maister classification is ingenious and useful. However, it begins to break down as soon as the authors introduce a second dimension by distinguishing between practice–centered business and business–centered practice, to yield six rather than three basic types of firms. The procedure ignores the correlation between dimensions, for example, the overwhelming tendency for strong–delivery firms to also be business–centered practices and for strong–idea firms to be practice–centered businesses. As a result some classes of firms in their system are artificial categories which probably do not correspond to firms in the real world.

should only go after projects it has a good chance of winning; to do otherwise is regarded as an inefficient expenditure of office resources. However, marketing personnel on the staff of firms say that 25 percent of the projects their offices pursue are a waste of time. They attribute this to the egotism of principals who continue to yearn for jobs that will offer an outlet for their design imagination or will bring professional prestige to the office. The terms of the criticism make one wonder if marketers really understand the architectural temperament.[13]

Organization clients use a wide range of techniques for choosing a firm or service to manage their space needs. The older tradition in which architects got their jobs through social and family contacts with a captain of industry or the benefactor of an institution continues to a limited degree in the private sector, especially for flagship buildings such as the national or international headquarters of a business. Personal contacts are still helpful in making the "short list," even though they do not provide assurance of a commission. Generally speaking, Coxe is absolutely correct when he writes: "there will always be some work awarded on personal favoritism…but the design marketplace has changed drastically in the last two generations, and today's clients demonstrate time and time again a high degree of openness to new approaches and new faces."[14] The procedures that are common now resemble the procedures used when purchasing any other expensive service or piece of equipment. In the large organization, staff members visit buildings comparable to those the clients contemplate erecting, go to trade shows, talk with other clients, look through the professional magazines, solicit brochures, welcome architects and other dealers who call on them, keep files on eligible firms, develop checklists for reviewing the competence of firms, and pursue other techniques along the same lines. Private corporations, including non–profit groups such as orchestra and museum boards of trustees, also have begun to stage invited competitions for four to six architectural firms. Juries for these elite commissions are typically composed of staff members of the client advised by leading practitioners and critics in the architectural community. The standard procedure now is that the firms invited to enter are paid a substantial advance fee for preparing submissions. Even so,

---

13. "Straight Talk from Straight Folks: America's Marketing Leaders Speak," *SMPS News*, 12, no. 2 (February 1987), pp. 3–4.
14. Weld Coxe, *Marketing Architectural and Engineering Services*, p. 84.

participants complain that the reimbursement provided often covers only one–third of their true expenditure.[15]

In the public sector, personal favoritism and the old boy network have almost completely disappeared, along with other remnants of the "spoils system." All levels of government now try to imitate the standards developed by the General Services Administration, which is required to advertise its intentions for projects, to consider all submissions, choose a panel of qualified firms at the regional level, review them according to stated procedures, and draw up a list of three finalists who are then chosen on the basis of professional qualifications by a national board of jurors. Frequent attempts are made in Congress to introduce the price of architectural and engineering services as a criterion for selecting among the three finalists. So far the AIA has fended off the effort, arguing successfully that making fees a criterion would result in price becoming the determinative factor, thereby diminishing attention to the quality of the building or service.[16]

The sum of the measures described in this and previous chapters puts the client in a stronger position than ever before in the history of modern practice to dictate to the architect not simply the services the firm is expected to perform, but more to the point, the services the firm will be *allowed* to perform. The process has also created tremendous difficulty for architects trying to clarify their identity and their role and position in relation to a specific building project. There is perhaps no place where the dilemma of professional image is revealed more clearly than in the glossy magazines directed at the audience of fellow professionals. Given the relentless competition architects face from each other, from other design professions, and from other types of companies that are now active in the building industry, it is not surprising that the major trade magazines play down the crucial role in the building process of non-architectural groups and other professionals. Standard accounts in the magazines make it difficult to determine the role of the associated local architectural firm in the design of the Humana headquarters building in Louisville

15. On the costs to architects of participation in private competitions, see Robert Gutman, *Design Competitions in the U.S.A.*

16. The latest effort, introduced by Rep. Berkley Bedell of Iowa, was withdrawn after protests by lobbyists for both engineers and architects. See "At Press Time." On the assumption that it will improve the quality of competitors' submissions for major projects, the GSA reimburses the three finalists who are selected to present preliminary designs. In 1978, when the program started up, the amount of the reimbursement was between $40,000 and $50,000. On the GSA procedure in 1978, see *Architectural Record*, December 1978, p. 34. Current procedures are discussed in U.S. General Services Administration, Office of Design and Construction, *Architect/Engineer Services*.

by Michael Graves; or the contribution of ISD, an interior design firm, to setting the decor of Johnson and Burgee's AT&T building. It is correspondingly difficult to find out the part played by the Gerald Hines interests, and the local Texas offices they employ, in the final design of buildings attributed to Graves, or Helmut Jahn, or Stern. Occasionally, as in science laboratory buildings designed by the Venturi firm, the respective contributions of Venturi and Payette are publicly acknowledged, because of the critical role performed by the technical systems in this building type, because both firms are architectural firms, and because the clients are public institutions. A similar acknowledgment of the division of professional labor will occur when two equally prestigious design firms are involved, as in the publicity for the new Equitable Life headquarters in New York City. Edward Larrabee Barnes designed the building, but the interiors were handled by Conway Associates, the interiors subsidiary of Kohn, Pedersen and Fox. In the case of Graves's Portland municipal building, the specific roles of the Graves firm, the contractor who was a joint venturer, an independent construction-management firm, and the Portland architects who planned the interiors of the city offices, were spelled out in full. In this case, too, one reason for the disclosure was that the client was a public agency. However, Graves also was determined that certain features of the finished building which did not meet his design standard, should not be attributed to him.[17] Except for such instances, the trade press, but even more so magazines such as *Architectural Digest* or the *New York Times Magazine*—whose editors regard architecture as if it were furniture, fashionable clothing, or gourmet cooking—ignore the complex relations among the cast of characters who now participate in a major building project.

The difficulty faced by the critics and journalists reflects the agony of the profession. Architects are tremendously confused about how to define their role in the building process in response to the increasingly aggressive stance in the process adopted by organization clients. The situation is different from the historic position of architects, in which the profession simply accepted the fact that there was a whole range of building types and tasks from which they would be excluded. Now, as we have seen, architects and firms are being sought out to an unprecedented extent. But along with the big growth in demand has emerged the resourceful client. Even though

---

17. Emory Roth and Sons was the associate architect. The contracting firm which participated in the competition bid was Pavarini Construction Co. Morse/Diesel was the construction project manager. Zimmer, Gunsul, Frasca Partnership was responsible for the interior design of the city offices.

such clients look to architects more frequently, they and their staffs are determined to define the scope of services precisely along with the conditions under which they will be provided. Opportunities for practice therefore are more numerous and more lucrative. But architecture is still a vulnerable profession defending itself against organization clients who more than ever before possess the ability to invade the domain architects had hoped to occupy unchallenged.

Competition With
Other Professions

That clients now undertake in their own behalf activities that many architects believe are in their domain, is a relatively recent development in the industry. The competition between architects and other professions for domination of the building process, however, is a contest with a long history, extending over centuries. Some leaders of the profession expected that the architect's position would become more powerful if the professionalization movement, which began during the 1850s, was successful. The goals of the movement were for architects to agree on one legitimate path to the achievement of recognized competence, by grounding the knowledge of design in science and reason and by teaching this knowledge in approved schools regulated by the profession. The success of the movement was to be measured by the adoption of licensing laws in each of the states of the Union. The purpose of these laws was to designate those men who should be regarded as fully trained and as possessing trustworthy competence for the design and supervision of building construction, thereby excluding other occupations and professions from working in the field.[1] The first licensing law for architects was established in the state of Illinois in 1897. This law, and similar laws in the other states, were supposed to secure for architects the exclusive right to design buildings "fit for human habitation." However, the anticipated result was not achieved. Architects design most of the major public and institutional buildings in the United States, such as schools, universities, museums, city halls, and airports, but are involved in the design of no more than 50 percent of the housing units and only about 30 percent of the commercial buildings.[2] These estimates are consistent with the way in which the state registration statutes handle the claims of engineers, who are the architects' principal competitors.

The astonishing fact revealed by the tabulation [of state licensing statutes] is that excepting those jurisdictions with a defini-

1. Some members of the profession opposed the licensing laws, on the grounds that architecture was an art, and that there was no way of licensing an art without the risk of diminishing the autonomy and individuality of the artist. Some critics of the profession in Great Britain have continued to oppose the registration system. See Malcolm McEwen, *Crisis in Architecture*, p. 60.

2. With the exception of the statistic for housing design, these estimates depend a good deal on informed guesswork. For the estimate of the profession's role in housing design, see Gutman, *The Design of American Housing*.

tion [of each profession]…every statute defines the practice in terms of doing certain things in connection with certain objects. With very few exceptions, the architectural statutes see those objects as buildings, structures, or appurtenances thereto. With very few exceptions, the engineering statutes see those objects as buildings, structures, or appurtenances thereto…It is a fair conclusion that in the preponderance of jurisdictions the engineers are entitled, under the definition of their practice, to do what the architect can do and a great deal more.[3]

Several cases have been joined between these two professions before state courts in the past decade. In many of them, the courts have ruled that there is a distinction between buildings used by human beings and other structures, and that the training of engineers does not give them as much background to design for human use as architects receive. However, the contest between architects and engineers for the right to be active in the building field continues. The laws of most states allow engineers to design buildings for habitation if they are incidental to a legitimate engineering design project, such as an electric power station or a factory. There is a consequent tendency, as the architects see it, for the engineers to take advantage of these clauses to extend the range of their work. Furthermore, registration statutes differ among the states and courts are sometimes unsympathetic to architects' claims for exclusiveness.[4]

Civil engineers are still recognized as the appropriate designers of bridges, tunnels, utility plants, and other structures where technical questions of loads and stresses dominate. There are certain building types for human habitation in which these issues are also critical, including skyscrapers and other tall buildings, and buildings with wide spans, such as stadiums and convention centers. Engineers who may defer to architects in the design of most building types, nevertheless

3. American Institute of Architects, *Survey of Laws Governing Registration of the Design Professions*, p. xiv. Also see Justin Sweet, *Legal Aspects of Architecture, Engineering and the Construction Process*, pp. 215–216.

4. I am grateful to Bartholomew Longo, Esq. for providing me with information and materials relating to the legal disputes between engineers and architects. Mr. Longo's firm served as the attorneys for the American Institute of Architects and the New Jersey Society of Architects, which together filed an amicus curae brief supporting the plaintiff, the New Jersey State Board of Architects, in a suit against a New Jersey engineer. The engineer had claimed the right to design a duplex house because of the unusual foundations it required. The court ruled in favor of the State Board of Architects. *123 A. and 456 (N.J. Super. Ct. App. Div. 1986).*

are trying to reclaim these large scale structures as the proper domain of their field. Their argument is based on the tradition of nineteenth century practice described in "The New Structure of Demand," in which architects whose education was in engineering, such as Jenney and Adler, were the authors of many innovations in skyscraper design; and on the modernist architects of the twentieth century who at least paid lip service to the "engineering esthetic."[5] The majority of engineers working on skyscraper design today serve as consultants to architectural firms or as partners and associates in architectural and engineering (A/E) firms. In these situations, most of the credit for the projects and the publicity is accorded to the architects involved, and increasingly so as attention shifts to the skin and outward appearance of all building types, including skyscrapers. The engineers understandably resent second-class status in the eyes of the public and the media, especially because without their expertise there would be no stadiums and skyscrapers for the architects to decorate. Also, they realize that in the industry as a whole, the top billings are earned by the AE firms and the engineering and architectural (E/A) firms, the offices in which engineers are also partners. These include such well-known comprehensive firms as Skidmore,

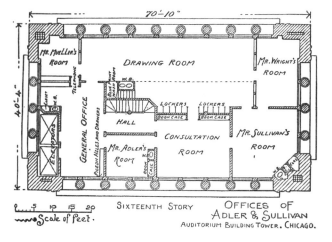

Figure 7. Floor plan of the office of Adler and Sullivan, Chicago, 1890. The illustration is of the sixteenth floor, the lower floor of their two–level office in the Auditorium Building. Frank Lloyd Wright, who was Sullivan's principle design assistant at the time, occupied the room in the upper right corner of the drawing.

5. An effective presentation of the point of view in the form of an argument on behalf of "structural art" is found in David Billington, *The Tower and the Bridge,* chap. 1 and Epilogue.

Owings and Merrill and Daniel, Mann, Johnson and Mendenhall.[6] In SOM's case, John Merrill, an engineer, was added as a limited partner three years after Skidmore and Owings, two architects, set up the firm. Merrill was recruited specifically for the purpose of enabling the firm to create and coordinate big projects.[7]

At the same time that the old dispute goes on between architects and engineers, other occupations are emerging which are pushing for recognition, and are having some success in taking over the architect's work. There are three such groups: persons trained in the visual arts; newer design professions, especially interior designers, and to a very limited degree, landscape architects; and professions and businesses that do not possess design skills but do have knowledge and experience dealing with other aspects of the building process.

The first group, the visual artists, includes painters and sculptors. The tradition of visual artists designing buildings goes back at least to Italian Renaissance cities—indeed most of the architects of the great buildings and palaces of these cities *were* painters.[8] It was feasible then for these artists to take on the task of designing buildings because the practical problems of erecting relatively simple building types could be handled by experienced groups of masons and other building craftsmen. If the building design was unconventional, as was the case in the first Gothic cathedrals or the domes of Renaissance churches, the painters and sculptors collaborated with master builders and amateur engineers of the period.[9]

The interior designers make up the majority of the second category of newer competitors. Like the engineers, they have a historic claim on the field. Beginning sometime at the end of the nineteenth century, women, in particular, who were discouraged from becoming architects or were excluded from architecture schools, began to design interior domestic spaces, often along with furniture. The concentration of women in the field during a century in which the principle of patriarchy dominated membership in the

6. "Design Billings Gain 12% in 1984."

7. "The Architects from 'Skid's Row,' " p. 210.

8. Richard Goldthwaite, *The Building of Renaissance Florence*, chap. 7.

9. Robert Mark discusses the collaboration as it applied to the design and construction of Gothic buildings in his book *Experiments in Gothic Architecture*, chap. 1. A comparable role is possible today for architects wishing to emphasize their artistic and painterly skills because of the efficiency of the modern building industry and the existence of the technical professions I described in earlier chapters. Their presence on the construction scene absolves the architect of the need to be familiar with many practical issues in building design or to deal directly with the building trades.

professions inevitably diminished the status of the interior designer.[10] This condition began to change with the rise of industrial design as an identifiable specialty in the 1920s, and the slow blurring of the lines between the design of domestic space by the interior designers and the design of work space by the industrial designers. In any case, interior design is now an established profession, with 23,000 members in the American Society of Interior Designers (ASID), educational programs in many universities, and several professional journals devoted to its accomplishments. It is still engaged in a battle to become a licensed profession, a project that is being vigorously opposed by the AIA. State chapters of the AIA are lobbying against registration for interior designers in every state in which it is being advocated. Architects are also pressing building inspectors not to allow any exceptions to codes requiring an architect's stamp on building permits.[11] As of July 1986, and in large part because of the architects' opposition, the title of interior designer was protected in only three states although such protection is reported to be under consideration in twenty states.[12]

The competition between architects and interior designers is probably more intense now than ever before in the history of architecture. Rivalry between the two professions results partly from the growing domination of the national economy by the service industries. These industries are housed in buildings that are more or less empty shells with indeterminate spaces: in such buildings the primary architectural effort is applied to the organization and decoration of the partitions, inside walls, furniture, and equipment. Because of high turnover rates of commercial tenants and the frequent changes taking place in the functions and relations among bureaucratic units, new interior designs are called for constantly. A related influence is the extensive conversion and rehabilitation of interior domestic space in loft and decayed apartment buildings in major cities. A study of economic activity in New York City during the first half of 1980 showed that these jobs made up half the construction projects begun in Manhattan during that period.[13]

10. Doris Cole, *From Tipi to Skyscraper*, chap. 4.

11. Stephen MacDonald, "Building Battle: Interior Designers Pitted against Architects in Licensing Dispute," p. 33.

12. American Society of Interior Designers, "Comparative Analysis of Acts Passed or Proposed" (mimeographed). As recently as the 1930s, several prominent architecture schools included departments and programs in interior design. Now, however, most interior design departments are located in other colleges of the university system.

13. Sharon Zukin, *Loft Living: Culture and Capital in Urban Change*, p. 130.

The interior space market is currently in flux. Work is split equally four ways, between consultants responsible to the architect; interior designers and architects working directly with the building owner; in-house departments which are in effect profit centers or subsidiaries in architectural offices; and in-house departments, including facility managers, in the client's organization. Kohn, Pedersen and Fox has a 70–employee interior design subsidiary, Conway Associates, which in addition to working on KPF's projects, also provides services to other architectural firms or does work independently for clients. A firm such as Gensler Associates of San Francisco, one of the first American architectural offices to specialize in space planning and interiors, is often chosen as the joint venturer when another architectural firm has the responsibility for the building shell. Architectural firms have more confidence in an interiors office whose principals are architects. Gensler Associates is now the biggest interior design firm in the United States, collecting total fees in 1986–87 of $32 million.[14] AT&T and Arco are examples of client organizations which have their own staffs for handling interior work. Until recently, AT&T's staff also operated as a profit center, marketing its services to other clients. IBM, on the other hand, is a big corporation that uses the full range of alternative design systems to cope with space planning and interior renovation. With the interior market so big now, and so many different types of services available, architects are focusing more on whether their firms run the project than on the specific educational background of the persons in the office who do the actual work.[15]

Many skills of men and women trained in landscape architecture overlap the skills of architects, and this fact generates competition between the two professions. Landscape architects and architects, however, generally respect each other's domain, to a much greater extent than do interior designers and architects. Architects have not opposed the registration of landscape architects, for example, as they now oppose state licensing for interior designers.[16]

Competition between *firms* of architects and landscape architects is somewhat more active. A few large offices, some of whose founders were trained in landscape architecture and acquired their

14. "CD and R's 200 Interior Design Giants."

15. "Survey on Architect Selection Revealed," p. 33.

16. Albert Fein, *A Study of the Profession of Landscape Architecture: Technical Report*, sect. 1, pp. 40-41. There are always a few architects who prefer to undertake their own garden designs, but there is almost no architect who will claim expertise in the major technical areas of ecological analysis, horticulture, and regional planning. These attitudes are reciprocated: landscape architects rarely undertake the design of buildings, except small structures.

initial reputation in this field, have gradually crossed over into architectural design through the route of "environmental design." Sasaki Associates in Boston and McHarg, Wallace, Roberts and Todd (recently restructured) are examples of such firms. Even these firms, however, concentrate their work at the scale of land development and regional planning, and leave the task of building design on their projects to architectural offices, or to partners and associates who are licensed architects. An important reason why there is not greater competition between landscape and architecture firms is that the locus of employment of landscape architects traditionally and still today is in municipal, county, state, and federal government agencies. In 1970, 40 percent of landscape architects were working for different levels of government.[17]

The third group of competitors to the architectural profession are the building professionals. The group includes contractors, construction managers, producers of industrialized buildings, and facilities managers. Members of these occupations are probably the principal source of competition now, and also are the group most likely to increase their activity. I discussed the participation of these competitors in earlier chapters. It is important to emphasize the sense in which this group challenges architects, because it covers a limited area. Building industry professionals generally do not compete in the realm of design. This is confirmed by the fact that the AIA, which so far has refused to endorse legislation to register or license interior designers, has supported the program to license construction managers.[18] On the contrary, managers and specialists in building usually employ trained and licensed architects (and sometimes other design professionals) to handle their design work. Some of the architects they hire are firms of independent professionals. In other cases, architects become their salaried employees. The ground on which the building professionals do pose a challenge to architects is in taking over functions of management and supervision before, during, and following construction, functions that architects often have defined as their responsibility. In so doing, the building professionals inevitably diminish the total volume of work for architects compared to what it would be otherwise.[19]

17. Ibid., table p. 13a.

18. "Survey Indicates Preference for Licensing of CM's." The views of architects on this question are just the opposite of their stance toward interior designers.

19. The market for architectural services is also reduced, but very slightly, by the right of owner–occupiers to design their own buildings, providing these are simple structures and can be built for relatively small sums ($50,000 or less in most northeastern states). These are mostly houses. The law is written this way to benefit farmers and other residents of rural areas.

It is difficult to assess the general outcome of the battle among the professions, to determine who is gaining ground and who is losing it. It varies with the competitor (and, of course, with the building type, the client, and the region of the nation). Architects have probably won the contest with the painters and sculptors. Very few visual artists without architectural degrees are actively engaged in building design as a regular career. The only visual artist currently renowned as an architect is James Wines, head of the architectural firm SITE, Inc., who originally practiced as a sculptor. Civil engineers have probably lost ground as designers of buildings for human use over the last one hundred years, although they are active as consultants to architectural firms in their own specialized realm.[20] There is a good deal of effective competition from interior designers, but then, as I said, architectural firms are much more active in the field, too. The major loss for architects has been in the areas of the building process outside design. In this realm, they have been losing jobs to package dealers, construction managers and contractors. But this loss is critical because so much of the economic and political power over building projects, and therefore over design, is concentrated in these functions.

When architects contemplate their future, they may well take heed from the experience of interior designers. One reason for the low esteem of interior designers in the past was that they were seen as having a purely cosmetic role. Indeed, interior designers were known until recently as "interior decorators." In the past few decades they have begun to take over the functions of space planners and facilities managers. In these roles they have developed the capacity to address many of the practical issues of building use.

20. Francis Ventre, an experienced analyst of professional trends, has argued that the share of design fees going to engineering firms has been increasing relative to architectural offices. He concludes from this that "engineering firms [are] increasing their influence over building investment decisions." However, Ventre's conclusion ignores the changing mix of types, in which the construction of buildings traditionally within the design province of the architect is diminishing relative to structures conventionally regarded as the domain of civil engineers. In the period covered by Ventre's analysis, 1967 to 1977, the dollar volume of multifamily housing and non–residential or commercial building construction declined from $43 million to $36 million. These are building domains that architects dominate. On the other hand, the areas that engineering firms dominate—single–family dwellings, industrial plants, water supply facilities, and highways, tunnels, and bridges—increased in dollar volume from 47 million to 114 million over the same period. For Ventre's analysis, see "Building in Eclipse." Information relating to construction receipts by building types for 1967 is in Gutman, Westergaard, and Hicks, "The Structure of Design Firms," tables 24 and 27. Data for 1972, 1977, and 1982 are reported in the Census of Construction Industries for those years. U.S. Department of Commerce, Bureau of the Census, *Census of Construction Industries*, 1972, vol. 2, table 8; 1977 and 1982, Summary Volume, table 11.

Nevertheless, they still suffer under the burden of their previous iden-tity and their lack of experience in dealing with the design of the building shell. The architecture profession is still some distance from encountering the image and identity problems of interior designers, but in the case of some firms, not very far removed. The willingness of many practitioners to accede to the preference of clients that the architect should limit his or her work to decorating the shed, poses a threat to the profession's competitive advantage. So does the ac-celerating loss of responsibility to other groups in the building in-dustry. Together these two developments present a dreary prospect that should be a more pervasive concern of the profession than it now is.[21]

21. I am grateful to Barbara Westergaard for making me sensitive to this danger.

Competitiveness Among Architects

The growing competition between architects and other building and design professionals is now matched by growing competitiveness among architects and architectural firms themselves.

The evidence in support of the view that competitiveness has increased is considerable. For example, both architects and clients agree that many more firms are active in seeking any one job than was common even a few years ago. The trend is visible in the private sector, where firms are regularly engaged in soliciting work, and where, too, they are being welcomed by purchasing departments and managers of facilities divisions who are determined to develop less risky, more rational methods for allocating commissions.[1] Competition has also increased in the public sector. The Public Building Service, for example, reports that there has been an increase of 10–15 percent over the last ten years in the number of firms that respond to RFQ announcements (Requests for Qualifications). The growth rate in the number of responses accelerates when the private sector construction economy is slack.[2]

The increase in the number of jobs in which architects are chosen through a formal "competition" system, making use of a selection jury that includes other architects, is another sign of increased competitiveness. Between 1,500 and 2,000 architectural firms and individual architects now regularly enter such "competitions." Some of these contests are restricted to architects working within a particular region, but others are open to entrants from the whole country and from abroad. Most of the entrants in open competitions are young architects who teach or who have steady employment in offices. However, there is a special category of competitions that are entered by large and well established firms, with nationwide practices. These competitions are known as "invited" or "limited" competitions, in which sponsors preselect four to six firms who have the skills and experience to handle the project. These are the type of competition mentioned in "The Organization Client," in which entrants are guaranteed reimbursement for some of the costs accrued in develop-

1. The only reasonably well documented study of current procedures used by architects to get work deals with practice in Great Britain. See Godfrey Golzen, *How Architects Get Work*.
2. Private communication to the author, November 6, 1986.

ing their documentation. I recently estimated that the number of competitions in the United States, including open, limited, and invited competitions, increased by 1,000 percent between 1975 and 1985.[3] This big growth is related to the expanding supply of architects, and to the discovery by sponsors that competitions are an inexpensive and sometimes efficient method to select an architectural firm.

The impact of the competitive spirit on the morale of the profession, and on the manner in which practice is conducted, has been enormous. Probably the most conspicuous effect is the emphasis the average architectural firm now puts on organizing its "business development" program, including marketing and public relations efforts. It is estimated that there are 4,000–5,000 full-time employees in U.S. architectural firms who manage and implement these programs. Some are architects, others have degrees in engineering, but probably the majority find jobs in architectural firms following a work background in other types of producer service businesses. These specialists keep track of prospective clients, arrange meetings for their architects with clients, organize presentations, prepare firm brochures and newsletters, organize publicity, stimulate newspaper coverage of building events, and do whatever else may be required to make sure the firm's name and accomplishments are known to potential clients and the public.

Self-promotion is an old tradition among architects and is connected to the dependence of architects on patrons and clients for the realization of their ambitions. Can one "fancy a painter unable to make pictures except when someone says to him: Paint now, paint this or that, and paint it thus and so." Unfortunately, architects are almost always in this position, because as critic Van Rensselaer adds, "architecture is not an art pure and simple. It has a practical side."[4] This may be one reason architects talk so much about "autonomy." In any case, the persistence with which the search for clients is now undertaken and acknowledged to be necessary *is* a relatively new

3. Gutman, *Design Competitions in the U.S.A.*
4. Mariana G. Van Rensselaer, "Client and Architect," p. 260.

development.[5] Marketing programs first emerged in discussions of architectural practice during the 1930s, and, in other industries, were recommended as a strategy for surviving the Great Depression. Royal Barry Wills, a stock plan architect and designer of villas and modest suburban houses, took up the theme in a book he published in 1931 on the business of architecture. In it, he included a section advising his fellow professionals about how to "stalk and capture" clients.[6] The decade of the 1930s was when the brochure developed as a device for promoting firms. A sleek brochure prepared by Louis Skidmore for SOM, around the time of the New York World's Fair, was one of the first.[7] Marketing programs took their next big leap during the construction recession of the 1970s. Many comprehensive firms, such as Hugh Stubbins and Sasaki Associates in Boston, SOM in New York, and RTKL in Baltimore, all firms with several hundred

Figure 8. Partners of Skidmore, Owings and Merrill, visiting retired partner Louis Skidmore at his Florida home in the spring of 1957. Skidmore is at the extreme right. Clockwise around the table, beginning at his left are: William Hartman, Nathaniel Owings, John Merrill, Gordon Bunshaft, James Hammond, Robert Cutler, John Rogers, Walter Netsch, J. Walter Sevringhaus, William Brown, Elliott Brown, Edward Matthews, and SOM lawyer, Marshal Sampselle.

5. The emphasis in this sentence must be on deliberateness and openness, since the problem of getting the job has long had a priority in practice. According to a famous story often told about Richardson, "a wide-eyed mother implored [him] one day, to advise her son who aspired to be an architect. 'What,' she asked, 'is the most important thing in architectural practice?' 'Getting the first job!' Richardson replied. 'Of course that is important,' she agreed, 'but after that what is the most important?' 'Getting the next job!' was Richardson's gruff response." William B. Foxhall, ed., *Techniques of Successful Practice for Architects and Engineers*, p. 101.

6. Royal Barry Wills, *The Business of Architecture*.

7. The brochure was designed by a delineator hired away from Raymond Loewy. Nathaniel Owings, *The Spaces In Between: An Architect's Journey*, pp. 76-77.

Figure 9. Columbian World's Fair Exposition architects, artists, and officials, Chicago, 1891. Left to right: Daniel Burnham, George Post, M.B. Pickett, Henry Van Brunt, Francis Millet, Maitland Armstrong, Col. Edward Rice, Augustus Saint–Gaudens, Henry S. Codman, George W. Maynard, Charles McKim, E.R. Graham, Dion Geraldine. Sullivan, who was involved in the project, is not shown.

employees, found themselves suddenly either without work, or with a much smaller number of committed projects. In addition to adopting the standard strategy of laying off architects and other staff, they set up special management task groups, reorganized their operations, and undertook to identify "countercyclical marketing opportunities."[8]

According to a survey conducted among Florida architectural firms in the early 1970s, the average firm spends about 3 percent of its total indirect costs on "business promotion and development," with the medium-size firms spending more than this amount and the firms with big billings a smaller percentage.[9] The overall rate of expenditure is closer to 5 percent now, with some firms spending as much as 8–10 percent on their marketing programs.[10] Marketing is now so commonplace that no architectural firm can afford to forego spending some funds in this area. Programs have been established by "avant-garde" architects, one– and two–person practices, firms that win design awards and those that never do, design-oriented offices, and highly commercial firms. Indeed, one sign that an avant-garde firm, such as Venturi, Rauch and Scott-Brown, Michael Graves Architect or Hardy, Holzman and Pfeiffer Associates, has become a recognized firm on a solid financial footing, is the presence of

8. "Survival in a Down Market: Lessons from the Past."

9. The estimate is derived from a study of 86 architectural firms in Florida in 1973-74. Florida Association of the American Institute of Architects, *The Economics of Architectural and Engineering Practice in Florida*, table II-3. The survey was conducted by Case and Company of San Francisco.

10. "Insurance up 33 Percent in One Year," p. 23. In 1987, Sasaki Associates of Boston was spending 8 percent of gross revenues on its marketing efforts.

marketing and public relations personnel on its staff and its use of consultants for this purpose.

In addition to in-house marketers, there are between forty and sixty consulting organizations that offer guidance and advice on marketing policy and procedures to architects, and several other organizations that give advise on and conduct public relations activities. Most of these organizations are one– or two–person operations, although Coxe Associates of Philadelphia, the largest and best–known firm in the country, lists thirteen associates on its letterhead. Three newsletters are published regularly on the subject of marketing and related subjects: *A/E Marketing Journal, Professional Services Management Journal*, and *Society for Marketing Professional Services (SMPS) News*. *Architecture, Progressive Architecture*, and *Architectural Record* allocate an increasing percentage of their text to reporting developments in marketing. Advertising by architectural firms in magazines that are read by staff members of client organizations, such as *Building Economics* and *Corporate Design and Realty*, which covers the office building market, is also becoming more popular. Books, manuals, and tape cassettes are put out by publishers of journals, by consulting firms, and by the AIA. These are targeted to cover the specific marketing needs of large firms, small offices, new firms, established firms and any other relevant category that consultants and publishers can identify. Most of the men and women active in the marketing and public relations field, including the staff of consulting firms, are members of the Society for Marketing Professional Services. SMPS has 4,000 members. Its annual convention is addressed by representatives of all segments of the building and design industry, who give talks or conduct workshops with titles such as "Reach Out and Qualify Someone: Successful Cold Calling" or "Blood, Sweat and Brochures."[11]

Increasing competitiveness among architects is manifested, too, in the growing number of firms that invade regional markets that were formerly considered the province of local firms. In the last quarter of the nineteenth century, architects of the stature of Richardson, Olmsted, Sullivan, and Burnham occasionally received commissions in cities far from their home base, but these were exceptions. Currently this is a standard experience of many large commercial firms and also of smaller offices specializing in the art of architecture. The process of nationalizing architectural practice, indeed of internationalizing it, is made easier by the availability of commercial

11. These titles are taken from the program of the SMPS 1986 national convention, "Marketing Tomorrow Today."

clients and construction companies that are themselves active in many different regional and overseas markets.

The growth in competition is a consequence of many changes in practice discussed earlier. For example, the competition from other design and building professions induces greater competition among architectural offices. In trying to get jobs that otherwise might go to interior design firms, architectural firms end up confronting fellow architects. The increase in the supply of architects and the rise in the number of firms are also factors. Although the growth in architects and firms is partly a response to expanding demand, no one would go so far as to argue that there is a *shortage* of architects at the present time. Over the short run, demand seems to lag behind supply, and this has the effect of preserving a competitive environment within the profession. Firms also vie with one another because of pressure on profitability. Unfortunately, the need to take such action tends to reduce profits further for the average firm, if only because of the rise in indirect costs occasioned by marketing and business development.

It may be of some comfort to architects to realize that increased competitiveness and the necessity to respond by improved management and marketing programs characterize most professionalized arts. These conditions also apply to science-based professionals, such as physicians, who were always assumed to be more secure and dominant in their domains. For example, on the same day that the *New York Times* carried a story that dance companies were hiring management staffs and marketing assistance, it also reported that Mt. Sinai Medical Center, one of New York City's oldest and best–endowed hospitals, was initiating a multimedia campaign to fill its beds.[12] Advertising and associated public relations efforts are also becoming common among group medical practices and HMOs and for other prestigious professionals, including attorneys.

Two related events, which have had a dramatic impact on architectural practice and are a clear manifestation of the underlying dynamics that have encouraged the growing competitiveness within the profession, must be mentioned. The first was the signing of a consent decree by the AIA with the Department of Justice in 1972 which removed from its code of ethics any prohibition against price quotations for architectural services. Although architects frown whenever an office competes by offering to work for a lower fee, the consent

12. "Dance Boom Begets Management Corps: Marketing Used To Be a Dirty Word. Now It's de rigueur"; and "Mt. Sinai's Multimedia Campaign."

decree opened the way for competitive bidding.[13] The second event was the AIA's approval in 1978, on a temporary basis, and then in 1980, permanently, of the right of members to operate as contractors on a building project they designed. The consent decree and the sanction of design/build practice marked a reversal of the AIA's century-old campaign to enlarge the architect's influence by segregating the architect's role from the business of building. In condoning design/build practices, architects seemingly forsook the symbolism of authority based on the ideal of professionalism, and instead legitimized the commercial side of architectural practice within the profession and in the legal system.

The movement to acknowledge the commercial aspects of practice was not supported to the same extent by all AIA constituencies. It was advocated most strongly by medium-size firms outside the metropolitan centers. These were firms that had a strong history of relatively secure practice, but that were also suffering most heavily from the competition of package dealers, and the penetration of regional markets by large offices based in the big cities. Smaller firms did not have the status and recognition, or for that matter, the financial resources of the large, national offices. The strong economic and professional position of the national firms allowed them to be neutral about the new commercialism and entrepreneurial emphasis. It was advantageous for them to operate under a veil of proper professionalism. The principal opponents to the revised code were one-person firms, or firms with just a few employees. These firms, which dominate the profession in terms of numbers but not in receipts, doubted their ability to obtain the credit necessary for a design/build practice. They clung instead, and perhaps naively, to the old-fashioned idea of a profession separate from the building industry.[14]

As a result of the changes forced upon the AIA to allow architects to also be contractors, adherence to the institute's code of ethics became voluntary. This arrangement met the requirements demanded by the Department of Justice (and was consistent with the preferences of many members), but it left the AIA without any code of conduct it could enforce. An occupation that wishes to maintain its

13. "Convention Delegates Vote 2–1 to Accept Justice Department Consent Decree," p. 47.
14. Larson and her collaborators are the first to have called attention to the skewed composition of respondents to AIA surveys, noting that the economic leaders of the profession are underrepresented and the small, struggling, one- or few-person firms are overrepresented. A similar skewed structure, reflecting the stratification of AIA membership in general, was active in the ethics debate. Larson, Leon, and Bolick, "The Professional Supply of Design," p. 275.

reputation as a profession cannot tolerate this condition for long. As a result, the AIA adopted a new mandatory code in 1986. It continues to permit architects to act as contractors and to have an ownership interest in projects. However, the code also requires architects to disclose to clients any potential conflicts of interest.

> If members have any business association, direct or indirect financial interest which could be substantial enough to influence their judgment in connection with their performance of professional services, the members shall fully disclose to their clients or employers the nature of the business association, financial interest, or other interest, and if the clients or employers object to such association, financial interest, or other interest, the members will either terminate such association or interest or give up the commission or interest.[15]

The new code is compatible with existing antitrust legislation as it applies to professional associations. However, whether it is sufficient, by itself, to control intraprofessional competition and modify the increasing emphasis in architecture on the marketing mentality and business acumen, is very doubtful. My guess is that the principal value of the code is as a renewed symbol of the ideal of professionalism.

---

15. American Institute of Architects, Canon III: Obligations to the Client. E.S. 3.2 Conflict of Interest.

Financial Problems of Careers
and Practices

The search for success in private practice runs up inexorably against the problems of ensuring the financial solvency of careers and firms. There is no other major profession in which practitioners confront these problems as regularly as architects. Take for example, the matter of architects' income. A study in the mid-1960s of the pre-tax compensation of principals in a representative group of American firms revealed that the average was 1.7 percent of gross revenues. Comparable figures for law and medicine were 8 percent.[1] Or consider the subject of lifetime earnings. A study of professionals in Great Britain conducted at the beginning of the 1980s indicated that not only were the lifetime earnings of architects below those of lawyers and physicians, they also were below those of university teachers and engineers involved in construction.[2] In 1982, the average starting salary in New York firms of recent graduates of top architecture schools was $15,000.[3] At the same time, graduates of law schools of comparable stature were beginning their careers at salaries of $40,000–45,000. It is no surprise, given this situation, that an architect who is concerned to make life easier for the younger generation than it was for his own cohort would say, "If I had a couple of million dollars in my pocket, the first thing I would do is go into real estate because I want to make the people who work for me happier by paying them higher salaries and I can't do that on architecture."[4]

The financial problems of firms are equally serious. Nearly one-half of the New York City offices that Blau interviewed in 1974 for her study of architectural practice were no longer in business in 1979. They were badly hit by the combination of the nationwide recession in construction and the municipal fiscal crisis. The vast majority of firms that failed had disbanded, although a few may have moved to other cities.[5] One could say that the failures were partly the result of the unusually severe cutbacks in private and

1. Case and Co., *The Economics of Architectural Practice*, pp. 57–58.

2. *Royal Institute of British Architects Journal,* December 1984, p. 7.

3. American Institute of Architects, New York Chapter, "Compensation Committee Report," p. 3.

4. Misner, "The A–Ds," pp. 95–96.

5. Blau, *Architects and Firms*, pp. 19 and 116.

public building projects resulting from New York City's borrowing difficulties. However, in every decade a severe downturn occurs in construction in one or another region of the nation. The high failure rate in architectural practice is consistent with the high bankruptcy rate in the construction industry generally. Even offices that survive the cyclical recessions and depressions in construction typically lose money on one-quarter of their jobs.[6]

In good times and in bad, the overall profitability of architectural practices averages 6 percent, calculated on net revenue and before the distribution of bonuses and the payment of taxes.[7] The most distressing fact, one that is bound to affect the structure of architectural practice in the future, is that profits for the typical firms have been declining since the late 1970s. Although the trend arises for specific reasons in architecture, some of the factors, such as clients providing more services in–house and larger expenditures on marketing, are obstacles shared with accounting, law, and other types of consulting firms.[8]

The decline in profitability overall is likely to accentuate differences between the general business strategy of the very large firms which remain profitable and are able to survive even in a down market, and the many smaller firms. These smaller firms live a hazardous existence. They are the most likely to fail in a recession; however, their flexible entrepreneurial style and willingness to try new clients and different approaches to design and practice endow them with greater profit potential when conditions are looking up. Using the theoretical perspective of the organizational sociologist, Judith Blau puts it this way:

> What is fail-safe with respect to organizational death but not particularly advantageous with respect to improving profits is a set of features that define the highly rationalized office: large scale, corporate affiliation, local projects, an aversion to using client networks, reliance on primarily corporate and government clients, and the use of outside consultants. These features are buffers against organizational death and allow firms to weather

6. Case and Co., *Economics of Practice*, p. 2.

7. Weld Coxe, "Myths and Truths about Compensation." Birnberg Associates, *1984 Financial Performance Survey for Design Firms*, p. 8.

8. David H. Maister, "Profitability: Beating the Downward Trend." The declining profitability of architectural firms is sometimes hidden by data that lump them together with engineering firms. A representative example of this kind of obfuscation appears in *Memo*, the newsletter of the American Institute of Architects, July/August 1986, p. 3.

the storm. On the other hand they do not enable firms to exploit new markets and thereby to advance their profitability.

Thus the fulcrum of risk in the case of failure and profitability depends on entrepreneurship. The flexibility of the small office is also their liability: they can tip either way. The established large firm, in contrast, is both unlikely to fail and unlikely to prosper.[9]

Architects are becoming more aware of the probable connections between styles of practice and profitability. With greater attention being shown to the economics of practice, the search for effective strategies of survival is bound to lead to still further fragmentation and differentiation among offices. This trend will make it harder to unite architects behind policies that address the problems of the profession. For example, less profitable firms already are reluctant to support the campaign to raise salaries and wages for recent graduates.

One can say that architecture has always been an unrewarding career in terms of income, for all but a very few practitioners, and is not chosen for its financial rewards. There is some truth to this argument. In a study conducted by the Association of the Collegiate Schools of Architecture in 1977, 70 percent of recent graduates reported that they were "satisfied" with their work activity, but 60 percent were "dissatisfied" with their earnings.[10] Many architects conceive of themselves primarily as artists. Beginning with the Romantic tradition, avant–garde artists did not expect to get rich. Principals and employees of many small firms that win, say, annual awards from *Progressive Architecture*, look on the field from a Bohemian perspective. It was partly because architecture was perceived as an art for which remuneration at commercial values was unlikely to occur, that it became a proper pursuit for a gentleman. However, ever since the professional tradition took hold in the middle of the nineteenth century, the average architect has expected to earn a respectable income. This was especially characteristic of American architects, even though many continued to regard themselves as entrepreneurs and dabbled in real estate development, at the same time that the new AIA was forging ahead with its attempts to make architecture into a licensed profession.[11] As we have seen, the contradictions within the professional establishment in the United States are still unresolved. It is noticeable that the contradic-

9. Blau, *Architects and Firms*, p. 124.

10. John W. Wright, *American Almanac of Jobs and Salaries*, p. 361.

11. Saint, *The Image of the Architect*, chaps. 4 and 11.

tion is now surfacing in Great Britain, too. The gentlemanly tradition was until recently so powerful there, that before 1979, the RIBA Code of Professional Conduct did not allow architects to initiate direct approaches to potential clients. Not only are direct approaches permitted now but a department of the RIBA advises members about marketing techniques and publishes a guide on the subject[12]

Poor compensation for architects, especially in the lower and middle ranks of offices, and the low profitability of the average firm, are serious matters. Over the long run, inadequate salaries are bound to discourage some very good talent from pursuing careers in the field. Very able graduates of some of the top architecture schools have gone on to study law, business, and medicine, even after obtaining professional degrees. The salary structure also affects where architects choose to work. Despite the many attractions of New York City as a center of architectural thought and culture, more young architects now avoid the city because their incomes are too low to cover living expenses and skyrocketing housing costs. This is probably a major reason why the New York chapter of the AIA has been the leader in calling attention to the compensation issue.

Relatively low wages and salaries are also among the conditions responsible for the high turnover rate in the staff of many firms, as architects seek opportunities which their current employers do not have the resources to match.[13] In addition to the distress moving from one underpaid job to another causes individuals personally, it also runs up the cost of conducting a practice. According to the report of the Compensation Committee of the New York chapter of the AIA, "losing an employee whose time is billable can cost 2–3 times the employee's annual salary in terms of lost time and retraining costs."[14] Turnover rates in private firms could well go higher in

12. Golzen, *How Architects Get Work*, introduction and passim.

13. Although good comparative data are not available, it is reasonable to expect that the volatility and vulnerability of the business of architecture should result in higher turnover rates than in law or medicine.

14. American Institute of Architecture, New York Chapter, "Compensation Committee Report," p. 3.

coming years. Increasing size and the bureaucratic personnel procedures of large firms lead many recent graduates to look for jobs that promise enlarged responsibility, or induce them to start their own offices. A teaching position in a school of architecture is often appealing for the same reason, especially when it serves as an income base from which to experiment with practice.[15] Furthermore, architects who have accommodated to modern forms of practice learn quickly that they can obtain higher salaries by going to work for corporations, construction managers, and real estate companies.[16]

The cost squeeze in private practice results from the obstacles firms face in raising their fees for services combined with the difficulty of controlling the expenses associated with practice. There are many reasons it is hard to raise fees, but one big factor is the availability of competing design and building professionals. Since the number of such competitors is increasing, the problem is likely to persist. A recent AIA study concluded that 70 percent of all major firms have engaged in competitive pricing at one time or another.[17] In response to the difficulty of achieving continuing profitability in regular practice, offices are turning to non–architectural activities. Profitable firms more and more are deriving a substantial share of their income from subsidiary or auxiliary activities. These activities include real estate development, design/build practice, and construction management.

Costs are being driven up, mainly as a result of increases in overhead rates, otherwise known as indirect costs. Direct costs, which include labor on a project and the fees for consultants, can usually be passed on to the client. This is important because consultants usually are remunerated at higher rates than architectural staff.[18] Overhead rates in the average U.S. firm, for example, have been increasing

15. Dana Cuff, "The Optional Academy," p. 14. Roger Lewis cites data to show that the salaries of teachers of architecture "are surprisingly competitive with the incomes of many architects in full–time practice, particularly those in smaller firms." Roger K. Lewis, *Architect?*, p. 141.

16. Ruth Hirsch, "Management: The Market for Architects." Employees of architectural firms who handle construction administration generally receive higher salaries than major design personnel, even though they have less architectural education, or none at all. The skills required for this kind of function are much in demand throughout the construction industry, and architectural firms who employ these personnel are competing with large construction companies. See American Institute of Architects, New York Chapter, "Compensation Committee Report," p. 3.

17. Society for Marketing Professional Services, *Distinguished Paper Series 1986*, p. 2.

18. According to the study of practice conducted under AIA auspices covering the period 1950 to 1966, there was a steady increase in the share of gross receipts that practices paid out to consultants. See Case and Co., *Economics of Practice*, p. 53.

more or less continuously over the past thirty–five years, and perhaps for a longer period. Between 1950 and 1966, they increased from 27 to 34 percent.[19] Measured in relation to direct labor costs, overhead increased from 133 percent in 1978 to 171 percent in 1984.[20] Although these statistics are taken from reports based on small samples whose representativeness cannot be determined, they are probably reasonably accurate in depicting a trend and are consistent with information about other producer service businesses. The principal components of overhead increases are the need to spend more on management, computer technology, liability insurance, research, and marketing. The cost of professional liability insurance alone increased 50 percent in 1986. Greater attention to principles of good management presumably results in more efficient practice and is emphasized to make sure that a larger portion of the expenditures of the firm can be charged to specific projects. Marketing is supposed to bring in more work, and work that will be more profitable. Both of these types of expenditures do not always achieve their intended purpose, however, and even when they do, it may take several years before the effects are discernible in profitability rates. Computer technology and insurance rates represent relatively new burdens. Especially among small firms, these costs sometimes transform a profitable practice into a money loser, which is one reason some small firms do not carry liability coverage.[21]

Just as there is no longer a single model of practice that all architects try to follow, so there is tremendous variation in the economic situation of firms. Although the financial history of the average firm and the income experience of the average architect are sad tales, some firms and their principals and top associates have substantial incomes. The same surveys, for example, that indicate the profitability of the average firm is 6 percent, also show that the top 10 and the top 25 percent of architecture firms have profitability rates of 22 and 14 percent respectively. The more profitable firms are those that have government rather than private sector clients, and are neither the very smallest or the very largest firms in the industry.[22] The complexity of the building types a firm designs is also a factor. One study of practice classified the commissions of firms in terms of six categories of complexity. They ranged from custom

19. Ibid., p. 49.

20. Birnberg Associates, *1984 Financial Performance*, p. ES–1.

21. "Practice: What Can We Do about the Liability Crisis Now?," "Hot New Market Lures A–E Players to Cutting Edge," p. 32.

22. Birnberg Associates, *1984 Financial Performance*.

residences, banks, churches, town halls, courthouses, museums, theaters, and country clubs, which were regarded as the most complex, to the least complex, including warehouses, storage spaces, lofts, barracks, and garages and service stations. The study concluded that the less complex building types were generally more profitable.[23] This seems to be the case even though for many jobs, particularly in the public sector, the percentage of total project cost awarded as fees, goes up as complexity increases. Principals in the more profitable practices reportedly earn between $99,000 and $134,000 annually, including salary and bonus.[24] In 1986, among the firms ranking in the top decile in terms of annual billings, principals' incomes of $200,000, including salary and bonus, were common.[25] Thus it appears that even though architecture generally is not a very remunerative profession, it is for some individuals and firms.

There is considerable discussion now in professional circles about the importance of raising salary levels, especially for younger people just coming into the profession. It is clearly a laudable goal. If achieved, it would probably help reduce the cost of private practice through bringing down the amount of employee turnover and the high rate of emigration by architects to related occupations and industries. On the other hand, the chances are small that architects in the average private firm will be paid much better than they are now, given the data on declining profitability and the entrenched factors causing this situation. However, the bigger and better established firms do pay higher salaries and wages than their smaller counterparts. The average salary of a department head in a New York City office with six to ten architects on the staff was $31,500; in a firm with twenty-one to forty architects, it was $35,846; while firms with over one hundred architects paid $43,480.[26] To the extent that the bigger firms increasingly dominate practice, this trend will benefit the profession as a whole. However, the firms that will be able to offer better salaries are also the firms that many architects do not like to work for, because of the management practices necessarily associated with bigness and bureaucratic settings. Their convictions are confirmed by sociological studies of practice. To quote Judith Blau again: "...that very structure on which [architectural] ideas

23. Case and Co., *Economics of Practice*, pp. 30–37 and 44.
24. Coxe, "Myths and Truths," p. 56.
25. Professional Management Services Journal Executive Management Salary Survey, 1987. Cited in *SMPS News* 12, no. 6 (June 1987), p. 4.
26. American Institute of Architects, New York Chapter, *1981 Compensation Survey*.

depend [in order] to have consequence is composed of the main conditions that disadvantage firms in the market economy."[27] In the conduct of architectural practice the challenge still is to find a method that will link organizational effectiveness and the other conditions making for stability and financial success with services and buildings of the highest quality.

27. Blau, *Architects and Firms*, p. 111.

The Public's Relation
to Architecture

Any discussion of the changing context for practice requires consideration of the public's role in architecture and decisions about architecture. Although architecture is perhaps more accessible than the other arts to knowledge and judgment by all, this aspect has acquired a renewed and revised significance with the growth of the modern democratic welfare state and the advent of advanced capitalism with its emphasis on stimulating consumption.[1]

The modern democratic welfare state affects architecture in three ways. First, the state is an owner and sponsor of buildings. The types of buildings governments choose to build, where they choose to locate them, the methods they use to select architects, and the architects they finally commission, all establish norms and ideals that other clients and building sponsors often imitate. The influence of government building programs is magnified because the federal government is the largest single client for buildings in the nation. In 1984, it spent 15 percent of all the funds expended on construction, and its share was even greater in previous decades. The Public Building Service alone is responsible for 7,200 owned and leased buildings encompassing 227 million square feet of space.[2] Furthermore, most government buildings are literally *public* buildings, open for use by citizens and highly visible. They often raise the most in-

---

1. For the purposes of this discussion, I omit from the category of the public all architects, building owners, and others whose livelihood derives from architecture and building. Obviously, architects and other members of the architectural community are citizens, and therefore, part of the public; but their relationship to architectural production is different from non–professionals. On changes in types of professionalism in the United States since the early nineteenth century, and its implications for the professional's connection to public questions, see Thomas Bender's discussion of the distinction between "civic professions" and "disciplinary professions." Thomas Bender, "The Cultures of Intellectual Life: The City and the Professions," pp. 183–84. One of the criticisms currently made of architects, and other professionals, is that they are insufficiently concerned with the well–being of the public.

2. In 1981 federal construction expenditures were equal to 22 percent of the total value of new construction. The percentage of the nation's total construction budget directly financed by the federal government has declined since 1981. U.S. Department of Commerce, Bureau of the Census, *Construction Review*, March–April 1985, p. 3. Information about the Public Building Service is from *ENR*, April 4, 1985, p. 36.

triguing kinds of design issues, and are, therefore, especially appealing commissions to architects.

Second, the state influences building and architecture through laws and administrative codes regulating architectural production. These affect some of the same issues influenced by the government's building program, but whereas the latter influences architectural ideas and standards indirectly, codes and laws lead to direct regulation of the nation's entire range of architecture and building production. Some codes and laws endow architects with professional status, and therefore constitute the basis for their authority. Other laws limit this authority by regulating the location of buildings, by setting zoning envelopes that shape architectural forms, and by specifying amenity standards, ranging from the educational facilities to toilets.[3]

The modern welfare state is the most aggressive and insistent regulator of the built environment history has ever known. Even in the present era, when deregulation of the economy is a popular political doctrine, the scope of environmental regulation has hardly diminished.[4] As a consequence, the number of rules professionals are expected to respond to keeps increasing. In large architectural offices, involved in the design of many buildings, the task of keeping up with the details of codes is the full time responsibility of more than one staff member. I stated in the first chapter, the volume of regulation is a factor leading clients to hire experts and thus expands the architects' market. The growth of the regulatory system also offers the professional community an opportunity to assume a more active role in the formulation of regulations. The profession, however, is often ignorant of this opportunity. For example, architects did not originate or sponsor a single one of the 461 changes proposed for the 1984 Uniform Building Code.[5] On the other hand, the New York chapter of the AIA was deeply involved in 1981 as a critic of the city's new zoning code, for which some of its members had been technical consultants.[6]

Government involvement in architecture has also in recent years probably contributed to the increase of competition within the profession. The democratic state must operate through full disclosure, not only of jobs that are available, but also by making explicit the procedures it uses for selecting architects. Although disclosure has been a

3. There are many examples of the connection between rules and policies promulgated by the state and the shape and content taken by buildings and urban environments. See Kenneth Frampton, "The Generic Street as a Continuous Built Form."

4. The program of reducing the authority of the Occupational Safety and Health Administration (OSHA) over workplace environments is a possible exception.

5. "Architects Are Gearing up for Technological Literacy."

6. *AIA Journal*, May 1981, pp. 22–25.

principle regulating the operations of the federal government with respect to the selection process for a century, it was not until the passage of the Architect–Engineer Selection Act, widely known as the Brooks bill, in 1972, that agencies were forced to follow the principle. Now hundreds of firms that once thought they would never have a chance to design a major government building are responding to announcements by the General Services Administration, and are getting commissions.

There is a third category of state programs, which European governments have undertaken for many centuries, but which only recently has begun to be accepted as an obligation of governments in this country. This is the task of promoting, fostering, and encouraging interest in the art of architecture and concern for the esthetic quality of the built environment. The appointment of fine arts commissions in various cities toward the end of the nineteenth century, including the establishment of a fine arts commission in the District of Columbia, are precedents for state involvement in the United States.[7] The movement to select architects for federal buildings through the competition method and Department of Housing and Urban Development awards to public housing projects and transportation systems are other examples. The significant forward step in this category occurred in 1965 when, during the administration of President Lyndon Johnson, Congress passed legislation establishing the organization that later became the National Endowment for the Arts. Through its Design Arts Program, one of twelve programs devoted to the advance of different arts, the NEA encourages competitions, initiates demonstration projects in design and urban innovation, supports worthy designers with innovative ideas, and encourages research on design problems. During the 1970s, the National Endowment for the Arts advocated greater use of competitions in both public and private buildings, even as heads of other government departments and the leadership of the AIA opposed it.[8]

---

7. Lois Craig, *The Federal Presence*, p. 252.

8. In testimony to a Congressional subcommittee on building needs, Admiral Marschall, Commissioner, Public Buildings Service of the GSA, said that he believed that competitions extend the time of selection and thus cost the government more money. Randall Vosbeck, president–elect of the AIA, voiced total opposition to design competitions for federal projects. U.S. House of Representatives, Hearing before the Subcommittee on Public Buildings and Grounds, July 1, 1979, *Public Building Needs*, pp. 159–62 and 261–63. The testimony by the NEA staff in favor of competitions is given in U.S. Senate, Hearing before the Committee on the Environment and Public Works, October 15, 1979, *Architectural Competitions*. It is important to realize that the state's role in fostering the arts is not universally applauded. See Edward Banfield, *The Democratic Muse: Visual Arts and the Public Interest*.

The development of government involvement in architecture has been accompanied by greater interest in questions of environmental quality and good design among the citizenry, the public–at–large. However, in the American case, the attention to architecture and a better environment is specifically the result of advanced capitalism, which has generated a large, affluent, well-educated group of middle-class men and women who are concerned about preserving and maintaining healthy and safe surroundings and who also are fascinated by well-designed artifacts that offer sensory delight and function as status symbols. The interests of this class are manifested at two levels: in their roles as users of buildings and environments, and as consumers of the architectural culture.

It is important to realize that the environmental movement and the attraction to high culture are largely middle– and upper–class activities. The lower one descends on the scale of social status, the less frequently one is likely to find people who are active in the user and consumer movements that relate to architecture. For example, it is significant that American trade unions have not devoted nearly so much effort to the quality of the work environment, except with respect to safety, as have unions in European countries. In Sweden and Germany, legislation now requires that employers consult employee unions for their view of design proposals before building plans are approved. There is no comparable legislation in force in the United States.[9] However, it is interesting that managers in many private corporations and institutions solicit worker and staff views about space requirements and environmental preferences. The policy is implemented most fully for buildings in which professionals and other upper–white collar personnel are employed, such as research laboratories, teaching hospitals, and corporate headquarters buildings. Indeed, another function of facilities managers whose role I discussed in "The Organization Client" is to serve as intermediaries between users and architects, contractors, and higher levels of management, conveying information about employee requirements to those who are involved most directly in planning new facilities. One of the reasons behind management's concern is the belief that designs that are more responsive to worker needs will improve productivity and morale.

The public also displays more interest now than it did in the 1970s in the condition of housing and housing–related environments. The renewed interest reflects the rise in the cost of providing satisfactory housing, the growing pedestrian and vehicular density in the more

9. Peter Jokusch, "The Changing Office—Some Recent German Developments and Issues," in Dolden and Ward, eds., *The Impact of the Work Environment*, p. 61.

popular central cities such as New York, Chicago, and San Francisco, and the extent to which the problems of the homeless and the poor have begun to invade the space and perceptual field of the privileged classes. Also, given the fact that most city dwellers spend more time in their neighborhoods than in the places where they work, housing environments affect the entire family. The majority of Americans dwell in owner–occupied housing, which gives them an economic stake in the outcome of the decisions of regulatory authorities. In addition, in the American tradition, there are well–known and established social norms and procedures that favor and encourage citizen participation in debates about the housing environment. A good example of increasing involvement is the growth in public attendance at hearings on matters relating to building and zoning. This increase is most noticeable in suburban communities, but it now also occurs in large cities and among apartment dwellers. The views expressed by voters concentrate on issues of amenity value. It no longer is simply a matter of the height of buildings, the width of streets, the availability of sidewalks, and access to parks and other green spaces. Public opinion now plays a part in decisions about the landmarking of districts, and the preservation of historic buildings. In major metropolitan cities, the views of citizens now encompass relatively recondite aspects of design, as is revealed by recent disputes about the esthetic acceptability of proposed additions to the Whitney and Guggenheim museums in New York City. Local opponents to the proposals for both museums have drawn upon the rhetoric of the neighborhood ideal and call themselves "Neighbors of the Whitney" or "Guggenheim Neighbors." Their use of an urban planning concept to mask a choice based at least in part on a stylistic preference reverses the traditional relationship between esthetics and planning.

More attention by building users and communities to the architecture surrounding them has had diverse impacts on practice. In some respects it has worked to expand the demand for the services of professional experts. For example, community protest about the proposal to build an addition to the Guggenheim has had this effect: the ensuing publicity has led not only to more jobs for the Gwathmey–Siegel firm, but for Kwartler Associates, who were hired to develop a counter proposal, as well.[10] Also, the interest of the middle class community in preservation has operated to encourage the incorporation of historical forms into contemporary building, and thus helped to foster the popularity of some post–modern styles.

10. The counterproposal by Kwartler Associates is illustrated in *Oculus 3* (November 1986), pp. 4-6.

However, while the volume of work for certain firms may be greater because of these movements, clearly they have also increased the number of groups who are legitimately able to intervene in the design process, and thus have had the effect of undermining the architect's autonomy and control. As a result, the idea of increased user participation in the design process, particularly participation in the early stages of the process, is met with mixed reactions by architects. Some architects, especially those who were in school during the late 1960s and early 1970s, are ideologically committed to the principle that an important criterion of good design is how well the building fits the requirements of workers and inhabitants. They tend, therefore, to welcome maximum user participation. There is also a group of clients who are impressed by architects who demonstrate professional concern for the acceptability of a building to successive groups of tenants and users. These clients believe that buildings and spaces that users admire preserve their economic value longer. In turn, some firms regard explicit interest in the response of users as a marketing tool, which can result in a higher level of repeat business than the standard rate for the industry of 50–70 percent.[11] However, many architects resent the addition of still another layer of opinion to an already overburdened and painfully slow review process, especially as it has functioned recently for institutional and government buildings. Apparently citizens believe they have a greater right to modify these projects than they do buildings being constructed by developers and private corporations. However, architects are reluctant to express their complaints openly, since as professionals, they are supposed to be spokesmen for the public, representing its interests.

The consumers of architecture are a wide range of people. They include a small group who hires fashionable architects to design its villas, apartments, or offices; and a much larger number of men and women who are not building owners or even heavy users of them, but who like to read about architecture, tour buildings, visit museum exhibitions, buy architectural drawings, and discuss architecture. One might call the second group "architecture buffs." The characteristic that defines them is that they all want a personal relationship to the esthetic dimension of architecture, for the delight and satisfaction it can offer, without having the burden of dealing with the practical problems of buildings as artifacts. They are really consumers of the "culture" of architecture.

---

11. Nydele, "Practice," p. 51; and Blau, *Architects and Firms*, pp. 109–11 and 158, n. 14.

The significance of the consumers of architectural culture for the practice of architects is that they create an alternative market, one that is not immediately tied to the building industry. Indeed, given the extreme fluctuations in construction demand, combined with the inclination of developers and other clients to circumscribe and control the activities of architects who design buildings, this market offers the prospect of considerable autonomy.

There has been a tremendous expansion in opportunities to consume architectural culture over the last few decades. Twenty–five to thirty American museums now have important architectural collections, including drawings and models. There are five of these in New York City alone.[12] The availability of guidebooks about the architecture of major cities and regions of the United States is another token of the culture market. More than twenty–five guides are now in print, including books about the architecture of Boston, Buffalo, Chicago, Detroit, Los Angeles, New Haven, New York, Philadelphia, San Francisco, and Washington, D.C..[13] New York City has several galleries that specialize in exhibiting and selling architectural drawings, a development that has helped to encourage the assembly of several important private collections of architectural drawings. Since the early 1970s, three American publishers—MIT Press, Rizzoli Publications, and Princeton Architectural Press—have established programs partly or wholly devoted to the production of books on architecture. Other companies, especially the university presses of Yale, Chicago, and the University of California, have been making conspicuous additions to their lists in the field. There are eight to ten bookstores in the United States specializing in the sale of current publications on architecture and a growing number of mail order booksellers who specialize in out–of–print books. The leading bookstores are Hennessey & Ingalls in Los Angeles, William Stout in San Francisco, Prairie Avenue Books in Chicago, and Rizzoli, the Urban Center and George Wittenborn in New York. Since the late 1970s, we have seen the establishment of major international awards for architecture, which for the first time are made by groups and foundations independent of the professional associations. The most important of these is the Pritzker Prize, which is awarded for achievement in "architecture as a fine art." There is also a new prize for architectural criticism, awarded in London.[14] Other significant cultural events have included the establishment of national and inter-

12. Jacques Cattell Press, *American Art Directory*, 1984.

13. *Books in Print*, 1985.

14. The national AIA, and local chapters, have, of course, awarded honorific prizes for a much longer period, as has the National Institute of Arts and Letters.

national study centers on architecture, the growth in enrollment by non–professional students in undergraduate courses in architecture and architectural history, the continuing swarm of applications to schools of architecture, and the presentation of major programs on

Figure 10. This advertisement for Dexter Shoes with a testimonial by Michael Graves is a sign of the celebrity status of architects. It appeared in several national magazines, including Time, Newsweek, and Sports Illustrated, in the autumn of 1987.

public television devoted to architecture and architectural personalities.

There is no question but that architecture has captured the interest of a broad public, that it has become a topic that is reported on and discussed in the daily press, the weekly magazines, and television; and that it is a subject about which the masses now hold opinions. According to the press office at the AIA, thirty newspapers in the country have writers or critics who cover architecture on a regular basis. Most of the activities I have mentioned would not be launched and could not be sustained if there were not tens of thousands of Americans who are prepared to buy books, take tours, and patronize exhibitions.[15] In addition, many members of the public are attempting to incorporate tokens of the architectural culture into their surroundings, on a scale they can afford. One result of this ambition has been a new interest in architect-designed central city lofts, designer furniture, fabrics, teapots, jewelry, and interior decoration. The interest extends outward, leading corporations to attend to the visual quality of the work environment, and giving a new lease on life to movements on behalf of improving product, industrial, and graphic design.

Many interpretations have been given of the explosion of public interest in architecture. As in the other arts, it is often regarded as evidence of the increasing maturity of American culture, in which appreciation of esthetic values is no longer confined to an upper class but extends to many more groups in society. Writing in 1936, the social economist Walter Kotschnig foresaw this development. In his book about professional unemployment during the Great Depression, he wrote that "the voice of the architects is all the more likely to be heard, as with 'America's coming of age' the appreciation of aesthetic values is spreading to new strata of society."[16] It has been said about the fascination with architecture that it fills a void in the new leisure class's demand for something to do and think about; or stated less pejoratively and with greater sympathy for the problems of living in modern society, it has become a preferred medium of self-expression and self-realization. Beginning with the commentaries of Veblen at the very end of the nineteenth century, attention to the arts was viewed as a manifestation of the social ambition of the cap-

15. These market-generated activities are supplemented by subsidies from many different sources, including individual donors, foundations, and local, state, and federal governments. The National Endowment for the Arts, for example, made a grant of $700,000 to the Public Broadcasting Service to produce the series *America by Design*, written and narrated by Prof. Spiro Kostof of the University of California at Berkeley. The series was first screened in 1987.

16. Kotschnig, *Unemployment*, p. 267.

tains of industry to create an American aristocracy. More recently, expansion in the production of art, including architecture, has been interpreted in terms of the principles of capitalist economies. These economies, so the argument runs, must constantly generate new services and commodities to commercialize and sell, leading to the development of a separate industry that produces and markets arts and ideas, often referred to as the "culture industry." Karl Meyer, for example, reports on the growth of subsidiary businesses and professions whose profits and income depend on the consumer market for art and architecture. In addition to those architects who purvey the ideas of architecture but do not design buildings, and the publishers and writers on the subject, there has developed what Meyer refers to as a "cultural bureaucracy," cadres of officials who administer arts budgets. At the end of the 1970s, there were 600 community arts agencies, of which no fewer than 85 percent had been organized since 1960; arts councils in most of the states; and 250 federal or quasi-federal programs of assistance to the arts, varying from the Air Force program of commissioning paintings for its art collection to the program of the Public Building Service to spend a fixed proportion of construction costs of new buildings on works of art. The magnitude of the post-war explosion in culture is indicated by the fact that in the thirty years following 1950, $61 million was invested in art museums and art centers with an aggregate size of 10.2 million square feet, or the equivalent of 13.6 Louvres.[17] According to Meyer, since 1950, this country has spent more money for the visual arts than in the preceding 150 years, and in so doing it has probably outspent the rest of the world besides.

The emergence of a mass public for the architecture culture is a phenomenon about whose benefits professionals will disagree. Everyone favors the attention that is lavished on architecture, which it is widely believed will assist in lifting the social position and prestige of the architect. But for some professionals the development of an audience disposed to consume architecture apart from the experience of building is linked to an excessive emphasis on the scenographic as distinguished from the stereotomic and tectonic aspects of architecture. In turn, some critics believe, this reinforces the image of the architect as a decorator rather than as a professional competent to deal with the pragmatic aspects of building, and thus accentuates, rather than revises, the direction in which practice is moving. Many other architects, however, accept the validity of scenography in architecture, and have established their practices to

17. Karl E. Meyer, *The Art Museum: Power, Money, Ethics*, pp. 73–75 and 127.

respond to this definition. The debate is linked to the arguments between post-modernists and modernists. The post-modern architectural style has profited from a culture of consumption. The modernists believe that the consumer view of architecture violates the unity of design with technology and the program. They regard it, therefore, as a self-inflicted threat to reviving and maintaining a comprehensive role for the architect in the building process. Given the threats which are already being generated by clients, builders, construction managers, package dealers, and competing professionals, one can ask whether it is necessary for architects themselves to exacerbate the problem.

Challenges to Architecture

I have described ten major conditions that form the context for architectural practice, and that have been undergoing significant transformations. They include (1) the extent of the demand for services; (2) the structure of demand; (3) the oversupply or potential oversupply of entrants into the profession; (4) the new skills required as a consequence of the increased complexity and scale of building types; (5) the consolidation and professionalization of the construction industry; (6) the greater rationality and sophistication of client organizations; (7) the heightened intensity of competition between architects and other professions; (8) increased competition within the profession; (9) the difficulties of achieving profitability and obtaining sufficient personal income; and (10) greater intervention and involvement on the part of the state and the wider public in architectural concerns.

These changes have been a source of anxiety and strain to architects. To the degree that individuals and firms have begun to acknowledge the new reality, the profession has been able to redefine the changes as challenges that should be confronted forthrightly. Some methods architects have developed have been very effective. Other challenges the profession has ignored. Still others, even when addressed responsibly, induce new conflicts and problems. Five challenges that are especially salient now in the consciousness of architects are discussed below, along with comments on the profession's response to them.

Challenge I. The need to match the demand for practitioners to the supply of architects, and to adjust the number of architects to the potential demand for their services.

Architects are in the fortunate position of being able, like other service professionals, to convince prospective clients of the need for their services. To this extent, there is a system in place that helps to make demand responsive to supply. On the other hand, it is important to realize that this process is effective to only a limited degree. I have discussed many other factors, besides the marketing efforts of architects themselves, that have an impact on demand.

There is an interesting point here to consider. Compared, say, to physicians or lawyers, architects are in a weaker position to generate demand for their services. They have nowhere near the authority over the building industry that physicians enjoy in the medical care system; and they do not have as much influence over building rules and decisions as lawyers can exert through the courts and the legislative system. Furthermore, when architects are effective in helping to pass laws or encourage the adoption of public policies that stimulate construction, the design work often goes to other professions. Despite their relatively greater power, lawyers and physicians, especially physicians, have taken measures over the past fifty years to limit the number of students who study for their professions. Meanwhile, the architecture schools are admitting as many students as university budgets allow. Perhaps the absence of measures by architects to restrict enrollment and the limited control they are able to impose on forces influencing the demand for services, are connected events. In both cases, the evidence points to a profession that has difficulty regulating its position in society.

Another aspect of the demand–supply relationship is worth noting. Principals who run firms find it to their advantage to maintain a substantial flow of architects through the schools. It provides offices of all sizes with an inexpensive supply of young graduates who are well educated but nevertheless are prepared to do low–skilled work. Although architects are embarrassed by their pay levels compared to other old and established professions, without the reserve supply of cheap labor the profitability of firms would be below the current rate. Physicians have dealt with the problem by setting up a system of internships and residencies, and by overseeing the establishment of other licensed professions, including nursing and pharmacy. These subsidiary professions are arranged in a hierarchy, which doctors regulate and which do not threaten their hegemony. Lawyers have been moving in this direction through recognizing a cadre of paralegals. Architecture once approximated such a system when practitioners controlled education by means of the apprenticeship and pupilage programs. Now that education is handled independently through university-based schools, the profession appears to be less, rather than more, capable of forming this kind of clearly stratified hierarchy. If the profession were able to establish such a system, it could go a long way toward reducing the dangers inherent in a prospective oversupply of graduates, raise salaries and wages throughout the profession, and also probably stem the downward tide of profits. However, my guess is that architects will never be able to introduce this degree of rationality into the organization of the profession's work. The nature of architecture as an art, along with the architect's image of individual creativity, inhibits the development of the division of labor associated with such an undertaking. The artistic identity is also a reason why the unionization movement is almost totally absent in the profession.

Unionization is proving a very effective method for adjusting the supply and remuneration levels of professionals to the demand for their services, but architects resist it. Even during the worst years of the Great Depression, when most architects were without regular work, fewer than 1,000 of the nation's 20,000 architects joined the Federation of Architects, Engineers, Chemists and Technicians. A leader of the Federation remembers them: "The architects were a pretty good group but they were pretty badly organized, pretty badly fragmented. They were individualists. They were a good group because they had a social consciousness."[1] At the present time the class consciousness of salaried architects is unawakened. Only 1 percent of architects working in the private sector are union members, and these are professionals working for non-architectural organizations. The percentages are larger among physicians and lawyers.[2]

Challenge II. The need to develop a philosophy of practice that is consistent but that also corresponds to the expectations, requirements and demands of the building industry.

The concept of a philosophy of practice covers a range of concerns: methods by which jobs are obtained; types of jobs undertaken; the division of responsibility between the office and other firms and organizations in the building industry; modes of organizing work in the office; and the place assigned to esthetic and formal issues in building design.

A reasonably consistent philosophy is important at two levels. First, with respect to the individual firm, a philosophy of practice functions as a guide for dealing with recurring problems, such as forging a plan for the firm's development, acquiring a distinctive image and attaining a specific niche in the market for services. It also smoothes over problems that arise within practices around questions of management, recruitment, and employee incentives. Second, looking at the profession as a community of firms, it can be argued that a shared viewpoint is also an advantage. It can assist architects in thinking about their identity. A more clearly conceived self-image can help to resolve doubts about the profession's proper role in the building industry. In turn, the resolution of uncertainty in this area should enable the architectural community to choose an effective strategy for dealing with other building professions. The AIA in particular, exhibits repeated difficulties in handling this problem. It appears to be unable to develop a consistent policy for dealing with

1. Tony Schuman, "Professionalism and Social Goals of Architects, 1930–1980."
2. Richard B. Freeman and James L. Medoff, "New Estimates of Private Sector Unionism in the United States," p. 162.

interior designers and engineers, and it is very unclear about the stance it should take with respect to the increasing power of building firms and developers. The inadequacies of the AIA necessarily must be a source of major concern. It is the principal official spokesman for the architectural community.

Consistent attitudes toward practice are hard to find among architects because of the variety of pressures influencing them, and the tremendous difficulties involved in finding a secure position in the marketplace. Even so, one is more likely to discover such a set of attitudes in individual firms, very much so in firms that have been able to attain, and then preserve, an influential position in the industry; but it certainly is not a characteristic of the whole architectural community. Commentators on the history of professions tell us that "faction is the distinctive feature of architectural politics," more conspicuous than in any other profession. However, there are many more such "cliques and coteries" within the community than in previous periods and the spectrum of attitudes displayed covers a wider range.[3] The variety is partly the result of the sheer volume of firms and architects who have a voice. However, it is also connected to the conditions of practice discussed in this book. These transformations have induced firms to pursue different strategies in order to survive and become renowned.

One reason prospects for the development of a consistent philosophy are much better in a single firm than in the profession, is that the firm is a small group. It can force out members who resist a consensus; or it can break up and start over again with a more compatible group of principals. Within the architectural community, there is no authority structure comparable to the power that principals hold in a private firm. This is also true for the AIA. As an association of professionals, it must mirror the concerns and preferences of its members, who in turn respond to the many different conditions under which practice is conducted. It is evident that the number of issues that are critical to the fate of architecture, on which the AIA can speak with one voice and take a stand, has been diminishing. The forced abandonment of its mandatory code of professional conduct for a period of almost a decade, is a telling sign of the decline of the AIA's influence on architects. Furthermore, although the AIA is the major spokesman for the profession, it is facing increasing competition from other organizations which claim they represent the interests of architects. These include the schools that grant professional degrees, the registration boards that are now

3. A. M. Carr–Saunders and P. A. Wilson, *The Professions*, p. 184.

organized into a national council, and, of course, the many clubs and institutes set up by practitioners in major metropolitan centers, and the independent architectural press. Each of these types of organizations has its own ideas about what the profession is, and what the aims of practice ought to be, which often deviate from the approach favored by the average firm constituting the bulk of AIA membership. The resulting diversity and heterogeneity contribute many positive benefits to the creative life of architects, but they also act as another force encouraging the fragmentation of the architectural community. The extent of this fragmentation is undermining the power of the profession within the building industry, and in its relations with clients and the public.

Challenge III. The need to maintain a secure hold on the market for services, in a period when the competition from other professions is increasing.

This need is a long-standing concern of the profession, for the reason that so much architectural knowledge and skill overlaps the expertise of other professions and occupations, including engineers, interior designers, surveyors, construction workers and managers, materials experts, and real estate economists. As I have pointed out, with the growth in the complexity of building projects, the competition from other professions and occupations is increasing. The individual architect cannot possibly keep up with the progress of knowledge in all the fields involved in the design and construction of a modern building.

In response to this difficulty, several strategies are pursued. First, the profession has welcomed the development of specialized training programs *within* the schools, so that there are now architects who are reasonably competent as architects *and* as building technologists, managers, and programmers. Second, and to an increasing extent this is the dominant strategy now, the profession has been transformed from a collection of self-employed practitioners into a community of *firms* staffed by salaried architects. Firms can make use of some of the principles of the division of labor, thus exploiting the knowledge of specialist architects and other building professionals.

A third strategy is also being used more frequently. This is for firms to concentrate in the one area where architects have claimed a special competence historically, and in which there is relatively little competition from other professionals who hold power in the building industry: the artistic side of architecture.[4] The popularity of this strategy is exemplified by the tremendous emphasis on design, to the exclusion of other professional services. The success of the strategy is related to the expansion in the consumption of "culture" discussed earlier. It is represented by the emergence of a clientele who relies on fashionable design and distinctive imagery to advertise and sell its products and services. The emergence of firms that function mainly as design architects, and sometimes indicate as much to clients, is a significant shift in emphasis from the attitude that dominated practice between the two world wars. During the 1920s and 1930s, it was more common for the leaders of the profession to argue that the key to survival was the ability to provide comprehensive services. The separation of the design function is not confined to simple projects and is not engaged in only by small "boutique" offices but is now a feature of the entire industry.[5] It is a development made possible by the availability of other practices that are prepared to handle the preparation of working drawings and specifications, deal with contractors, and generally supervise construction. On projects in which a design firm is located in New York, Philadelphia, Chicago, or Los Angeles and the project is in another state or smaller city, the combination of firms often meets other goals as well, such as giving the associated local firm responsibility for the review of shop drawings and site supervision.

It should be said that the tradition of specializing in the art of design is not without its precedents in the history of architecture, when the conditions of the building industry, the prescribed social position of architects, or the characteristics of a building type made it feasible. The architects of the Gothic cathedrals and other medieval buildings may have been master builders who knew a great deal about fabrication and worked along with the masons and carpenters on the site. However, many Italian Renaissance architects, students at the Royal Academy in London at the end of the eighteenth century, and nineteenth–century graduates of the Ecole des Beaux Arts in Paris, distanced themselves from the building

4. Gerald M. McCue and William R. Ewald, Jr., *Creating the Human Environment*, p. 280. Also see Magali Sarfatti Larson, "Emblem and Exception: The Historical Definition of the Architect's Professional Role."

5. The term "boutique economy" has become standard parlance in discussions of the changing structure of the American economy. It refers to the emergence of small specialized firms and companies that are said to be a source of technological innovation and are more adaptable and flexible in responding to market demand. "Boutiques" have become common in other producer service and professional businesses, too, including law and accountancy. Gail Appleson, "Boutique Firms Hold Their Own," p. 1. Also "Can America Compete?," p. 47.

trades as a mark of upper class status. The French architects have maintained a separate design tradition almost continuously from the time of Colbert. Still today, an architect in Paris or Lyon expects that construction drawings and building supervision will be handled by an independent enterprise, known as a "bureau d'etudes." The conception of a practice concentrated on design to the exclusion of other services, is a relatively recent development in the United States. It responds to a combination of conditions external to the profession, including the interests of clients in the art of architecture mentioned earlier, the greater specialization within the building professions, and a vastly more competent and technologically more advanced construction industry.

The problem of all strategies for coping with competition is that if architects know about them, they are also known by other groups in the industry. Civil engineers, builders, and contractors have tried to acquire a knowledge of the skills possessed by architects, and to use them. If they are not able to pick up the skills themselves, the large supply of architects turned out by the schools, and the desire of employees in big firms to moonlight, offer a ready supply of itinerant designers. Furthermore, interior designers are competent to deal with esthetic matters. Interior designers are now conducting practices that handle the shell and facade of buildings along with the inside scenery.[6]

There is no single method for fending off competition from other building professions. The "professional project," is a movement that began in the nineteenth century among lawyers, doctors, engineers, and other learned occupations to control their respective domains by securing an exclusive license to practice from governments. Although successful for some professions, the movement failed in terms of achieving the objective for architects.[7] It is true that only registered architects can use the title of architect. However, persons with other training and experience who work in the building in-

6. Since interior designers, even in the two or three states in which they are registered, are not licensed to design *buildings*, formal responsibility must rest with staff architects or professionals outside the firm. The practice of having third–party architects sign drawings for approval purposes is, of course, standard in many sectors of the building industry.

7. The concept of the professional project has received its fullest treatment in the writings of Magali Sarfatti Larson, especially her book, *The Rise of Professionalism: A Sociological Analysis*. Larson points out that there were many other methods through which professionals attempted to secure their control over a domain, in addition to obtaining a grant of authority from the state, including the construction of a definition of reality that would be accepted and believed in by clients. It can be said that one of the problems of architects is that they and their clients and users do not necessarily regard buildings from the same perspective.

dustry are allowed to perform many of the duties that architects would like to arrogate to themselves. Architecture remains, and is always likely to be, a highly vulnerable profession, although the various strategies that have been explored now and in previous periods will be able to improve the economic security and professional influence of some practitioners and some firms. Still, anyone who chooses architecture as a career must be prepared to endure a greater degree of risk in fulfilling his or her career aspirations than a person educated as a lawyer or a physician. In architecture, as in many other occupations, there are, of course, rewards other than a high income and job security that make the choice of the field attractive and worthwhile.

Challenge IV. The need to find ways to maintain profitability and solvency when the costs of running a design firm are steadily increasing.

It has proven extremely difficult to manipulate all the variables that determine the final profit and loss in an enterprise: to keep wages, salaries, and benefits down while attracting and holding onto qualified architects; to reduce other overhead costs; to maintain the level of staffing appropriate to a constantly fluctuating work load; to charge higher fees; and to discover new sources of steady income.

Three solutions have been widely advocated in recent years. First, to generate income from other sources, including construction and development subsidiaries. The revision of the mandatory AIA code of professional conduct has legitimatized the use of this approach. A second strategy is to manage projects and the work in the office more efficiently. Indeed, the belief in the value of better management as the key to survival and also to the achievement of high-quality performance is almost an obsession in the profession. It is exemplified by the appointment in 1984 of Louis Marines, an architect who had a career as a management consultant, to be executive director of the AIA. Third, to maintain a steady flow of jobs through the office, relying on marketing and public relations programs. More so than other types of producer service or consulting firms, architectural offices are either in a trough or are suddenly overwhelmed by tasks that must be completed in a great hurry. The volatility of the resulting work load can have a devastating effect on the organizational integrity of firms, not to mention a deleterious effect on profitability.

In some firms, one or more of these alternative solutions has been tried with magnificent results. There are several offices with reputations for design excellence or high-quality service, that are supported by profits from land speculation or housing and office development.

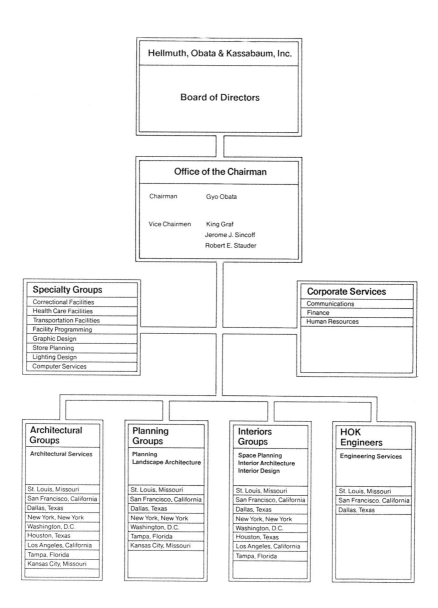

Figure 11. Table of Organization of Helmuth, Obata & Kassabaum, St. Louis, 1987. HOK is now one of the largest architectural firms in the world.

There are other well-known and respected firms that are very well managed, and as a result, their profitability has increased. These offices sometimes adopt a two-track method of operations. They produce dull, very efficient space for one group of clients, making use of their management expertise or their knowledge of how to make cheap buildings. However, the profit from these jobs is then used to underwrite losses on other projects in which superior design quality is the principal criterion. The surfacing of the marketing mentality in architecture, long after it became institutionalized in other producer service businesses, has been a boon to some offices whose principals once thought it was indecent to admit they hustled for work. Well-conceived, persistent marketing programs have fostered many newly affluent firms, and have probably contributed to the overall increase in the demand for architectural services. However, as I said in earlier chapters, there are some firms for which none of the strategies appear to work. They lead to heavier overhead expenditures and less profit, but do not result in additional business.

One difficulty in the application of conventional ideas about effective management to architectural practice has been the inability of firms and their consultants to understand the special characteristics of architectural work, and then to establish a philosophy of management appropriate to it. Architecture requires closer collaboration between personnel employed in advisory and management capacities and production workers than is necessary in almost any other service business. Most building jobs are unique undertakings, in which the organization of the design and building team must be defined de novo for each project. With their specialized technical knowledge, different team members are integral to drawing up the plan, just as they are essential for solving the problems that arise inevitably during construction. Because of the necessary collaboration between parties that in other industries are regarded as "management" and "labor," questions about the respective responsibilities of producer service personnel and production workers are often indistinguishable from substantive questions about the design of the project. The system of responsibilities and rights in the organization of the work group is therefore developed along with the building. This arrangement demands tremendous flexibility in patterns of authority, and a continuous process of exchange of power and influence between designers, managers, technical experts, contractors, and members of the building trades. It usually prevents the formation of the type of clearly established and acknowledged table of command that is standard elsewhere, and that management theorists so often advocate.[8]

The problem with the marketing approach is that, often in opposition to the purported aims that supposedly distinguish a professional organization from other producer service businesses, it leads architectural offices to put success in getting jobs ahead of dedication to the interests of users and the general public. This is not the intention of the advisors who have urged architects to become more proficient marketers. These consultants emphasize repeatedly that good service is a condition for effectiveness in selling. Nevertheless, the prevailing manifestation of the marketing mentality has been troubling for firms who are confused by how to balance professional values with profitability. The uncertainty seems to be intensifying, given the continued growth in the number of firms and the greater reliance on competitive pricing for getting jobs. To the extent that clients become aware that their architects are confused, and begin to suspect the depth of a firm's commitment to ideals of professional service, the result could be greater harm to the future status of the profession than several years of faulty management and mistakes in marketing.

In a profession as competitive as architecture has become, there is constant pressure to invent new approaches in order to stay ahead of the pack. However, managing and marketing consultants have spread their advice so effectively that different firms now use identical approaches, thus undermining the advantage each office hoped to achieve in formulating a strategy. Theodore Hammer, the managing partner of Hanes, Lundberg and Waehler in New York City, has commented on the irony of the situation.

> Clients are pretty smart. They've seen all the folks who have taken the [marketing] seminars come in and say, "We are truly dedicated professionals, we provide quality service on the budget, and we have a team coming off a project next week identical to yours." Then the other firm comes in and says, "We are

8. This discussion leans on a commentary by Piore and Sabel dealing with the conditions of work that encourage the preservation of fragmentation in the construction industry. I have revised and adapted it because it is such a good analogy to the operations of a design team. Michael Piore and Charles Sabel, *The Second Industrial Divide*, p. 117.

truly dedicated professionals..." Everybody sounds the same late-ly.[9]

It may turn out that the principal beneficiary of the doctrine that marketing programs can upgrade profitability is the business of the consultants themselves.

Challenge V. The need to have a competent organization exhibiting high morale and motivated to produce good work.

In all modern professions, a conflict develops between the demands of the organizations in which professionals work and the personal aspirations of individuals. This conflict is receiving increasing attention because so much professional work is done now in bureaucratic settings. These settings require routine work procedures and hierarchical structures for making decisions. Such demands clash with the expectation of professionals that they will be able to exercise the independent authority under which lawyers, physicians, and architects have traditionally operated. The sociologist Eliot Freidson has pointed out that even when they work in organizations, professionals are less subject to supervision and control than other employees. At the very least, professionals enjoy technical autonomy.[10] Nevertheless, it can be argued that the modern professional situation may be less conducive to responsible, creative work than when more professionals were self-employed and worked in smaller groups.

These conflicts may well be more common in architecture than in other types of professional practice. They emerge when architects work, as more of them do each year, as staff architects for corporations, real estate developers, and government agencies. Similar disputes also develop in professional offices run by architects. The tendency is accentuated by the special characteristics of architecture as a type of work activity. In the previous section I discussed the structure of the design and building team which demands close exchanges between service and production workers. These relationships inevitably challenge the standard formula according to which service businesses are managed. In addition, architecture attracts students who assume that practice permits an unusual degree of individualized, creative self-expression. These egotistic attitudes are encouraged in schools of architecture. The temperament of architects reinforced by educational experiences yields an employee population who probably are more prone than other professional

9. Society for Marketing Professional Services, *Distinguished Paper Series*, 1986, p. 21.
10. Eliot Freidson, *Professional Powers*, p. 166.

workers to insist on autonomy. Furthermore, the determination of design quality depends on informed, but intuitive, judgments. This method of evaluation limits the power of senior managers and administrators to impose their own standards on lower level employees. It is just this fear, that judgment based on status, age, and experience will not carry the weight that it does in other professions, that leads older architects and principals to adopt a dictatorial manner. In turn, younger architects are inclined to demand greater autonomy than they are capable of exercising.

The clash between the personality of many architects and the modes of thinking and managing required in practice contributes to the intensity of the debate about how to produce a combination of good staff morale and quality performance in an office. There is reason to think that this debate also is more prominent in architectural circles than in other professions. The argument is critical because the ideals of the profession tend to equate excellence in practice with design excellence, frequently ignoring the quality of professional service or the performance of the building. Design excellence often does result from providing relatively free reign to individual imaginations. As a consequence architects feel some kind of special responsibility to resolve the management dilemma in their firms.

There is no single correct method for attracting good designers, and motivating them to invest their work with significance and meaning. Staffing policies are determined by different objectives. These include the position principals wish to attain in the status hierarchy of the profession, the scale of projects on which they work, the range of services the firm provides, and the importance principals assign to maintaining continuity and reducing employee turnover. One might assume that firms celebrated for the design quality of their work would be good situations for architects with artistic talent, who would work happily and effectively in these settings. But it often turns out that such firms are dreadful employers for people who wish to exercise these skills, because the principals make all the interesting and important design decisions, while the majority of the staff is relegated to drawing up plans and details. Sometimes gifted designers do better in a firm with a strong commercial orientation, where their skills are more exceptional and therefore more highly valued. Firms that do small projects, including suburban housing developments, office buildings, and space planning, are frequently more stimulating environments for talented designers. The projects are simple enough so that principals are content to turn over major responsibility to junior staff. These offices may reproduce the atmosphere of old-fashioned ateliers, in which the principals serve as critics of schemes developed by young designers. However, because these offices are managed haphazardly, they often have a short life. If an atelier-type firm does survive and grow, it is usually as a result of having installed bureaucratic management techniques. However, as I have said, this is exactly the setting some of the best design architects abhor, and they then quit. In a comprehensive service firm, with its many projects concentrated on pragmatic issues, the morale of the designers may be poor, but architects proficient in technical skills may fare rather well. Principals usually allow employees more responsibility and authority than when design is the issue, because so many answers have become standardized and are routine. If the firm is large and successful, there may be opportunities for internal job mobility. We should not overlook the many architects who choose to work in technical areas for just this reason, even though their jobs do not receive the recognition from the profession or the public that is accorded to design tasks.

Various career paths and types of practice have been advocated as solutions to the motivational and organizational problems of principals and employed architects. There is no one method that can handle the diverse requirements of an increasingly complex, competitive, and fragmented profession with equal effectiveness. The combination of diversity and fragmentation are major factors that help to explain why architecture is populated by a higher proportion of alienated and disappointed men and women than any other major profession, why so many firms are badly managed, and why when offices are managed efficiently, they achieve work of dubious architectural quality. Of all the challenges facing the profession, the problems of motivating architects and sustaining office morale and performance may be the most difficult to address.

It would be nice to believe that the obstacles can be dealt with by a little tinkering: to find a more experienced marketing consultant, to separate the drafting room from the business office, to return to the model of the one-person or the two-partner office, to hire a new manager, to formulate an improved personnel plan, to recruit graduates from another school of architecture, or to acquire clients who are more appreciative and behave like patrons.[11] Each of these strategies has been tried by some firm and by individual architects. There are cases in which the adoption of such strategies has led to jobs which are more fulfilling and has improved the quality of work and the prospects of particular offices. But it is very unlikely that any

11. The suggestion about maintaining distance between drafting room (an older term for the place where design work is done) and the office is made by Morris Lapidus, *Architecture: A Profession and a Business*, p. 2.

one of these strategies can have a lasting impact, unless it is combined with significant shifts in career objectives, the patterns of office organization, or the backgrounds and experiences of the staff.

The problems of managing an architectural practice run too deep to be influenced by minor events and simple adjustments in the conduct of a career or a firm. Like the other challenges identified in this chapter they are rooted in the conditions discussed throughout the book. They are challenges that have arisen from great institutional changes that have occurred precipitously and intensively over the last fifty years, in the building industry, among different levels of government, in the corporate sector, and in environmental experiences of the entire American population. These changes have transformed the system of building production, the methods through which clients choose architects, the roles assigned to architects in the building process, and the standards according to which the merits of buildings are judged and architects and their firms evaluated. To deal with the challenges in coming decades, the adoption of ingenious management techniques by individual offices or the use of clever public relations programs by the architectural community, is unlikely to prove sufficient. Intensive research, thought, and policy initiatives focussing on these challenges are needed. To achieve these initiatives, the best minds and talents of the profession must be mobilized. But not only of the profession itself. Architecture is too important to the quality of American life for us to assume that the knowledge of architects working alone is adequate to address it. The issues and conditions this book has described demonstrate that architecture and building touch the interests of building owners, users, and the public at large. The production of architecture is achieved through the participation of clients, users, builders, manufacturers, other design professions, government officials, and financiers. These groups must be involved in the investigation along with the architectural community. Only if joint programs with this scope and on this scale are undertaken, is the profession likely to formulate persuasive policies that will assure the independence of architectural practice in future years.

Tables and Charts

Table 1

Distribution of Architectural Firms by Number of Employees, 1972–1982

Number of principals and employees	1972		1977		1982	
	#	%	#	%	#	%
All firms	10,179	100.0	10,954	100.0	12,110	100.1
0–19	9,492	93.3	10,387	94.8	**11,261**	93.1
20–49	531	5.2	435	4.0	619	5.1
Over 50	156	1.5	132	1.2	230	1.9

Sources:
    U.S. Department of Commerce, Bureau of the Census, *Census of Selected Services, 1972*, Subject Statistics, vol. 1, table 4.
    —, *Census of Service Industries, 1977*, Subject Statistics, vol.1, table 4.
    —, *Census of Service Industries, 1982*, Industry Series: Establishments and Firm Size, table 5a.

Table 2

Receipts of Architectural Firms by Size of Firm, 1972–1982

Number of employees	1972 $ ($1000)	1972 %	1977 $ ($1000)	1977 %	1982 $ ($1000)	1982 %
All firms	1,837,310	100.0	2,967,198	100.0	5,607,675	100.0
0–19	922,322	58.5	1,731,198	58.4	2,857,438	51.0
20–49	427,408	19.4	503,801	17.0	1,073,311	19.1
Over 50	487,580	22.1	731,818	24.6	1,676,926	29.9

Sources:
U.S. Department of Commerce, Bureau of the Census, *Census of Selected Services, 1972*, Subject Statistics, vol. 1, table 4.
—, *Census of Service Industries, 1977*, Subject Statistics, vol. 1, table 4.
—, *Census of Service Industries, 1982*, Industry Series, Miscellaneous Subjects, table 5a.

Chart 1a

Share of Receipts by Size of Firm: 1972

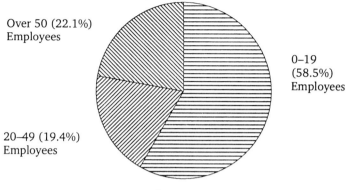

Over 50 (22.1%)
Employees

0–19
(58.5%)
Employees

20–49 (19.4%)
Employees

Chart 1b

Share of Receipts by Size of Firms: 1977

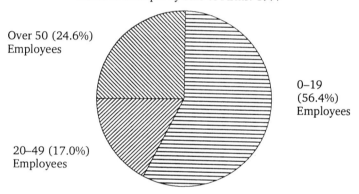

Over 50 (24.6%)
Employees

0–19
(56.4%)
Employees

20–49 (17.0%)
Employees

Chart 1c

Share of Receipts by Size of Firm: 1982

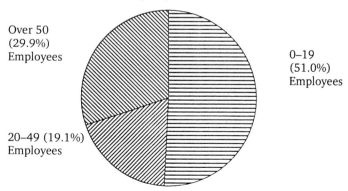

Over 50
(29.9%)
Employees

0–19
(51.0%)
Employees

20–49 (19.1%)
Employees

Table 3

Distribution of Architects according to Work Settings in Nine Countries, circa 1960

	1961 Belgium %	1960 Denmark %	1960 France %	1960 Norway %	1960 Portugal %	1960 U.S.A. %	1960 Finland %	1960 Hungary %	1964 Poland %
Private design firms	89.3	58.6	5.6	81.2	0.0	83.0	73.5	2.1	0.0
Construction industry	4.4	8.2	83.1	1.5	16.5	4.3	4.2	72.3	50.2
Other industries [a]	3.1	8.8	2.2	3.1	4.2	3.3	3.2	15.9	9.0
Institutions and government [b]	1.1	13.0	6.7	12.2	77.9	6.0	19.0	2.1	40.8
Total	97.9	88.6	97.6	98.0	98.6	96.0	99.9	92.4	100.0

Source:
Robert Gutman, Barbara Westergaard, and Cato Steegen, "Architects in Many Countries," table 4. Data obtained from United Nations, Economic Commission for Europe, *Handbook of Housing and Building Statistics*, tables 1B and 1C for each country.
[a] Other industries include architecture, mining and quarrying, electricity, gas, water, commerce, transport, and those where no adequate description is given.
[b] This category includes defense, public administration, government services, community, business, recreation, education, mental health, and personal.

Table 4

Receipts of Architecture Firms by Building Type, 1972–1982

Building type	1972	1977	1982
All types	100.0	100.0	100.0
Single-family dwellings	4.2	5.6	4.7
Multifamily dwellings	13.4	8.5	9.2
Commercial buildings	30.9	32.9	44.5
Water supply and sanitation facilities	0.7	1.1	0.8
Industrial plant processes and systems	3.9	4.3	4.6
Highways, roads, bridges, and streets	0.6	0.6	0.7
Airports and mass transportaton	1.2	1.9	1.9
Power generating and transmission facilities	1.6	0.6	0.5
Flood control, drainage, navigation, rivers, and harbors	0.1	0.2	N.A.
Naval and aeronautical	N.A.	0.6	1.6
Public and institutional facilities	36.0	36.6	26.6
Communications facilities	2.2	1.1	N.A.
Other	5.2	6.0	4.9

Sources:
U.S.Department of Commerce, Bureau of the Census, *Census of Selected Services, 1972*, Subject Statistics, vol.1, table 7.
—, *Census of Service Industries, 1977*, Subject Statistics, vol. 1, table 6.
—, *Census of Service Industries, 1982*, Industry Series, Miscellaneous Subjects, table 38.

N.B. Data for 1982 are from architectural *offices*, whereas data for 1972 and 1977 are from architectural *firms*, including firms with offices in more than one location.

Table 5

Number of Professionals in Specific Occupations, 1850–1980

Occupation	1850	1860	1870	1880	1890	1900	1910	1920	1930	1940	1950	1960	1970	1980
Architects	591	1,236	2,017	3,375	8,070	10,581	16,613	17,185	22,850	21,359	25,359	30,028	56,284	90,026[a]
Civil Engineers	412	N.A.	4,703	8,261	N.A.	20,068	39,730	56,060	87,586	84,607	123,600	159,809	178,334	202,253
Lawyers and Judges	23,939	34,839	40,736	64,137	89,630	114,460	114,704	122,519	160,605	179,554	172,290	209,684	277,695	527,243
Physicians and Surgeons	40,765	55,159	62,448	85,671	104,805	132,002	151,132	150,007	159,920	170,282	184,710	234,388	280,557	432,337

Source:

Data for 1850 to 1970 inclusive are taken from Robert Gutman and Barbara Westergaard, "Architecture among the Professions," tables 1 and 1a. Data for 1980 are taken from U.S. Department of Commerce, Bureau of the Census, *Census of Population, 1980, Subject Reports, Occupation by Industry*, PC80–2–7c, table 4; and Supplementary Report PC–80–S1–15.

[a]The number given in the 1980 census, 106,386, includes 16,386 landscape architects. See *Census of Population, 1980, Subject Reports, Occupation by Industry* PC–2–7c, table 4.

Table 6

Ratio of Professionals to Urban Population, 1850–1980

Ratio to 10,000 Urban Population

Occupation	1850	1860	1870	1880	1890	1900	1910	1920	1930	1940	1950	1960	1970	1980
Architects	1.67	1.99	2.04	2.39	3.65	3.50	3.94	3.17	3.30	2.93	2.67 2.62[a]	2.66 2.40[a]	3.77[a]	5.39[a]
Civil engineers	1.45	—	4.75	5.85	—	6.64	9.45	10.33	12.66	11.32	13.71 12.76[a]	14.13 12.76[a]	11.94[a]	12.11[a]
Lawyers and judges	67.62	56.01	41.15	45.39	40.54	37.89	27.27	22.58	23.22	24.02	19.12 17.79[a]	18.55 16.74[a]	18.60[a]	31.56[a]
Physicians and surgeons	115.16	88.68	63.08	60.63	47.40	43.69	35.93	27.65	23.12	22.79	20.49 19.07[a]	20.73 18.71[a]	18.79[a]	25.88[a]

Sources:
   Information relating to the number of professionals in each decennial year are taken from the same sources as the data shown in Table 5. Statistics of the urban population were obtained from U.S. Department of Commerce, Bureau of the Census, *Statistical Abstract of the United States, 1985.*

[a]The urban population was redefined for these years.

Chart 2

Ratio of Professionals to Urban Population, 1850-1980

Ratio to 10,000 Urban Population

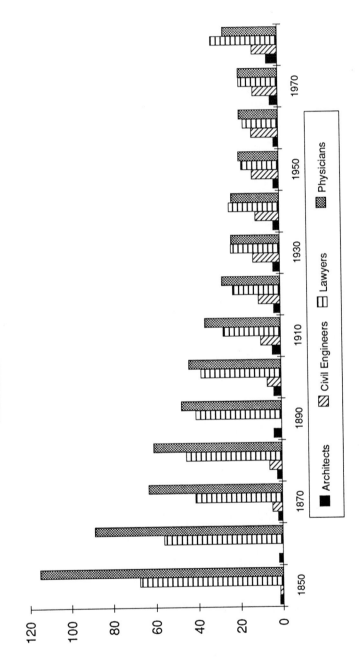

Table 7

Architectural Employment by Industry

Type of Industry	1960 #	1960 %	1970 #	1970 %	1980 #	1980 %
Total in all industries	30,028	99.9	56,214	99.9	105,079*	100.0
Agriculture, forestry, and fisheries	101	0.3	4,901	8.7	17,010	16.2
Mining	0	0.0	55	0.1	89	0.1
Construction	1,366	4.6	2,343	4.2	4,545	4.3
Manufacturing	961	3.2	2,289	4.1	1,716	1.6
Transportation, communication, and public utilities	242	0.8	744	1.3	1,126	1.1
Wholesale trade	41	0.1	238	0.4	313	0.3
Retail trade	243	0.8	460	0.8	1,552	1.5
Finance, insurance and real estate	362	1.2	793	1.4	2,877	2.7
Business and repair services	101	0.3	353	0.6	853	0.8
Personal services	0	0.0	208	0.4	162	0.2
Entertainment and recreation services	20	0.1	52	0.1	164	0.2
Professional and related services	25,340	84.4	40,498	72.0	69,587	66.2
Public administration	1,211	4.0	3,280	5.8	5,085	4.8
Industry not reported	40	0.1	0	0.0	0	0.0

Sources:
U.S. Department of Commerce, Bureau of the Census, *Census of Population, 1960*, Subject Reports, Occupation by industry, Final Report PC2–7C, table 2.
—, *Census of Population,1970*, Subject Reports, Occupation by Industry, Final Report, PC 2–7C, table 8.
—, *Census of Population, 1980*, Subject Reports, Occupation by Industry, PC 80–2, table 4.
*Includes approximately 16.000 landscape and naval architects.

Table 8

Total Enrollment in First Professional Degree Architecture Programs
47 Schools: 1930–1972

Year	Enrollment	Year	Enrollment
1930	4,535	1952	8,813
1931	N.A.	1953	9,213
1932	N.A.	1954	N.A.
1933	3,196	1955	N.A.
1934	2,896	1956	8,098
1935	2,657	1957	8,364
1936	2,754	1958	8,465
1937	2,964	1959	8,641
1938	3,235	1960	10,220
1939	3,453	1961	9,999
1940	3,617	1962	10,197
1941	3,531	1963	10,648
1942	3,471	1964	10,215
1943	1,499	1965	12,480
1944	2,628	1966	13,388
1945	6,293	1967	13,979
1946	9,004	1968	N.A.
1947	10,382	1969	13,586
1948	10,298	1970	14,314
1949	10,220	1971	14,905
1950	10,153	1972	13,757
1951	9,147		

Source:
  Vasco Fernandez, Robert Gutman, and Barbara Westergaard,
  "Enrollment Trends in Schools of Architecture, 1930–1970," table 1.

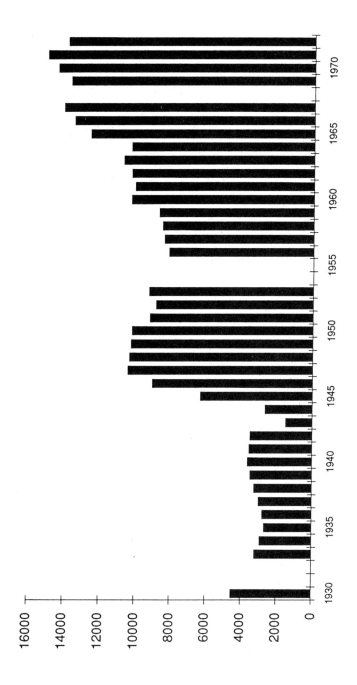

Chart 3

Total Enrollment in First Professional Degree Architecture Programs
47 Schools: 1930-1972

Table 9

Composition of the Labor Force of Architectural Firms, 1972–1982

	1972		1977		1982	
	#	%	#	%	#	%
Total employees	82,927	99.9	81,134	100.0	113,596	99.1
Licensed architects	26,052	31.4	31,464	38.8	39,681	35.0
Other licensed professionals	3,264	3.9	3,433	4.2	3,723	3.3
Technicians	28,591	34.4	27,074	33.4	37,683	32.2
All others	25,020	30.2	19,163	23.6	32,509	28.6

Sources:
    U.S. Department of Comerce, Bureau of the Census, Census of Selected Services, 1972, Subject Statistics, vol.1, table 4.
    —, Census of Service Industries, 1977, Subject Statistics, vol. 1, table 4.
    —, Census of Service Industries, 1982, Industry Series, Miscellaneous Subjects, SC–82-I–5, table 4.

Illustration Credits

1. Reprinted by permission from Richard Guy Wilson, *McKim, Mead and White* (New York: Rizzoli Publications, 1983), p.15.

2. Reprinted from *Pencil Points*, 5, no. 9 (September 1924), p. 84.

3. Photograph courtesy of Arthur Griffin.

4. Photograph courtesy of Robert Montgomery Brown

5. Photograph courtesy of Princeton University

6. Reprinted by permission from Mariana van Rensselaer, *Henry Hobhouse Richardson* (New York: Dover Publications, 1969), opposite p. 123.

7. Reprinted from *Engineering and Building Record.* 22, no. 1 (June 7, 1890), p. 5.

8. Photograph courtesy of Havendale Studio

9. Reprinted from Charles Moore, *Daniel Burnham* (Boston: Houghton Mifflin, 1921), opposite p. 100.

10. Photograph courtesy of Pagano, Schenck and Kay and Michael Graves Architect.

11. Chart courtesy of Helmuth, Obata & Kassabaum

Bibliography

Books and Articles

"AGC, AIA Tempers Flare over Conflict of Interest Issue." *Building Design and Construction*, 20, no. 12 (December 1979), pp. 46-47.

American Institute of Architects. *Architect's Handbook of Professional Practice*. Washington, D.C.: American Institute of Architects, 1963.

—. *Code of Ethics and Professional Conduct, 1987*. Washington, D.C.: American Institute of Architects, 1987.

—. *Design-Build/Contracting Monitor Task Force Report*. Washington, D.C.: American Institute of Architects, May 1981.

—. *Survey of Laws Governing Registration of the Design Professions*. Washington, D.C.: American Institute of Architects, 1970.

American Institute of Architects, New York Chapter. "Compensation Committee Report." *Oculus,* 3, no. 9 (June 1982), pp. 2-4.

—. *1981 Compensation Survey*. New York: New York Chapter, American Institute of Architects, 1981.

"Analysts Probe Design Firms for Keys to Market Valuation." *Engineering News Record,* July 19, 1979, pp. 23-24.

Applebaum, Herbert. *Royal Blue: The Culture of Construction Workers*. New York: Holt, Rinehart and Winston, 1981.

Appleson, Gail. "Boutique Firms Hold Their Own." *National Law Journal,* March 7, 1983, pp. 1, 22 and 23.

"Architects Are Gearing up for Technological Literacy," *ENR,* March 21, 1985, p. 46.

"The Architects from 'Skid's Row.'" *Fortune,* 57 (January 1958), pp. 137-40 and 210-15.

"Architects in Public Agencies." *Oculus,* 48, no. 4 (December 1986), pp. 3-27.

"At Press Time." *Building Design and Construction* 26, no. 12 (December 1985), p. 5.

Balmori, Diana. "George B. Post: The Process of Design and the New American Architectural Office (1868–1913)." Journal of the Society of Architectural Historians, 46, no. 4 (1987), pp. 342-355.

Banfield, Edward. *The Democratic Muse: Visual Arts and the Public Interest*. New York: Basic Books, 1984.

Banham, Reyner. *The Architecture of the Well-Tempered Environment*. London: Architectural Press, 1969.

Bannister, Turpin. *The Architect at Mid-Century: Evolution and Achievement.* New York: Reinhold Publishing Corp., 1954.

Bender, Thomas. "The Cultures of Intellectual Life: The City and the Professions." In John Higham and Paul Conkin, eds., *New Directions in American Intellectual History.* Baltimore: Johns Hopkins University Press, 1979, pp. 181-95.

Billington, David. *The Tower and the Bridge.* New York: Basic Books, 1983.

Birnberg Associates. *1984 Financial Performance Survey for Design Firms.* Chicago: Birnberg Associates, 1984.

Blair, William. "Should Architects Become Builders and Developers?" *New York Times,* August 10, 1980, sect. 8, pp. 1 and 10.

Blau, Judith. *Architects and Firms.* Cambridge, Mass.: MIT Press, 1984.

Blau, Judith, Mark LaGory, and John Pipkin, eds., *Professionals and Urban Form.* Albany: State University of New York Press, 1983.

Burgess, Peter G., ed. *The Role of the Architect in Society.* Pittsburgh: Department of Architecture, Carnegie Mellon University, 1983.

"Can America Compete?" *Business Week,* April 20, 1987, pp. 45-69.

Carey, Max L. "Occupational Employment Growth through 1990." *Monthly Labor Review,* 104 (August 1981), pp. 43-55.

Carr-Saunders, A. M. and P. A. Wilson. *The Professions.* London: Oxford University Press, 1933.

Case and Co. *The Economics of Architectural Practice.* Washington, D.C.: American Institute of Architects, 1968.

"CD and R's 200 Interior Design Giants." *Corporate Design and Realty* 6, no. 1 (January/February 1987), pp. 62-73.

"Century Development Corporaton." *Building Design and Construction* 20, no. 2 (February 1979), pp. 53-59.

Cole, Doris. *From Tipi to Skyscraper.* Boston: i press, 1973.

"Convention Delegates Vote 2-1 to Accept Justice Department Consent Decree." *Architectural Record,* 151, no. 6 (June 1972), pp. 47-49.

Cowan, Peter. "Studies in the Growth, Change, and Ageing of Buildings." *Transactions of the Bartlett Society.* London: London University, University College, Bartlett School of Architecture, vol. 1 (1962-63), pp. 53-84.

Coxe, Weld et al. "Charting Your Course." *Architectural Technology,* May/June 1986, pp. 52-58.

Coxe, Weld. *Marketing Architectural and Engineering Services,* 2d ed. New York: Van Nostrand Reinhold, 1982.

—. "Myths and Truths about Compensation." *Progressive Architecture,* July 1985, pp. 56 and 58.

Craig, Lois. *The Federal Presence: Architecture, Politics, and Symbols in United States Government Building.* Cambridge, Mass.: MIT Press, 1978.

Cuff, Dana. "The Optional Academy." *Journal of Architectural Education,* 40, no. 2 (Jubilee 1987), pp. 13-14.

—. *The Social Construction of Design.* Forthcoming.

Cullen, John. "Structural Aspects of the Architectural Profession." In Blau, La Gory, and Pipkin, eds. *Professionals and Urban Form,* chap. 11.

Cushman, Robert F. and William J. Palmer, eds. *Businessman's Guide to Construction.* Princeton, N.J.: Dow Jones Books, 1980.

"Dance Boom Begets Management Corps: Marketing Used To Be a Dirty Word. Now It's de rigeur." *New York Times,* February 24, 1987, p. C13.

"Deere & Company: Patron of the Architectural Arts." *Building Design and Construction,* 20, no. 2 (February 1979), pp. 53-59.

"Design Billings Gain 12% in 1984." *ENR,* May 16, 1985, pp. 36-38.

Dolden, Mary E. and Robertson Ward, Jr. *The Impact of the Work Environment on Productivity.* Washington, D.C.: Architectural Research Centers Consortium, 1986.

Downs, Anthony. *The Revolution in Real Estate Finance.* Washington, D.C.: The Brookings Institution, 1985.

Fabian, Thomas M. "Architects in Industry: Letter." *Crit,* Spring 1982, p. 34.

Fein, Albert. *A Study of the Profession of Landscape Architecture: Technical Report.* Washington, D.C.: American Society of Landscape Architects, 1972.

Fernandez, Vasco, Robert Gutman and Barbara Westergaard. "Enrollment Trends in Schools of Architecture, 1930-1972." Prepared for the Architectural Education Study, 1974.

Fitch, James M. "The Aesthetics of Function." In Robert Gutman, ed., *People and Buildings.* New York: Basic Books, 1972, pp. 3-16.

Florida Association of the American Institute of Architects. *The Economics of Architectural and Engineering Practice in Florida.* August 1974. Report of a survey conducted by Case and Company of San Francisco, Calif.

Foley, Patrick, Avner Shaked, and John Sutton. *The Economics of the Professions: An Introductory Guide to the Literature.* London: London School of Economics, April 1981.

Foxhall, William B., ed. *Techniques of Successful Practice for Architects and Engineers.* New York: McGraw-Hill, 1975.

Frampton, Kenneth. "The Generic Street as a Continuous Built Form." In Stanford Anderson, ed., *On Streets.* Cambridge, Mass.: MIT Press, 1978, pp. 309-337.

—. "Toward a Critical Regionalism: Six Points for an Architecture of Resistance." In Hal Foster, ed., *The Anti-Aesthetic: Essays on Postmodern Culture.* Port Townsend, Wash.: Bay Press, 1983, pp. 16-30.

Freeman, Richard B. and James L. Medoff. "New Estimates of Private Sector Unionism in the United States." *Industrial and Labor Relations Review,* 32 (1979), pp. 143-74.

Freidson, Eliot. *Professional Powers.* Chicago: University of Chicago Press, 1986.

Giovannini, Joseph. "The Grand Reach of Corporate Architecture." *New York Times,* January 20, 1985, sect. 3.

Goldthwaite, Richard. *The Building of Renaissance Florence.* Baltimore: Johns Hopkins University Press, 1980.

Golzen, Godfrey. *How Architects Get Work.* London: Architecture and Building Practice Design Guides, 1984.

Greenfield, Harry. *Manpower and the Growth of Producer Services.* New York: Columbia University Press, 1966.

Griffin, C. W. *Development Building: The Team Approach.* New York: John Wiley & Sons, 1972.

Gropius, Walter. *The Scope of Total Architecture.* New York: Harper, 1955.

Gutman, Robert. "Architecture as a Service Industry." *Casabella,* nos. 495/496 (1981), pp. 28-32; 108-9.

—. "Architects in the Home-Building Industry." In Blau, LaGory and Pipkin, eds. *Professionals and Urban Form,* chap. 8.

—. *Design Competitions in the U.S.A.* Published as an appendix to Great Britain, Ministry of the Environment, *Briefing Competitions.* London: Bulstrode Press, 1987.

—. *The Design of American Housing.* New York: The Publishing Center for Cultural Resources, 1985.

—. "Education and the World of Practice." *Journal of Architectural Education,* 40, no. 2 (Jubilee 1987), pp. 24-26.

—. "Patrons in Spite of Themselves." Prepared for the Workshop on the History and Sociology of Architectural Practice, School of Architecture, Princeton University, June 13-14, 1985. The paper is available from the author.

—. "Patrons or Clients." *Harvard Architecture Review: Patronage,* 6, pp. 148-59.

Gutman, Robert, Barbara Westergaard and Cato Steegen. "Architects in Many Countries." Prepared for the Architectural Education Study, 1974.

Gutman, Robert and Barbara Westergaard. "Architecture among the Professions." Prepared for the Architectural Education Study, 1974.

—. "What Architecture Schools Know about Their Graduates." *Journal of Architectural Education,* 31, no. 2 (1978), pp. 2-11.

Gutman, Robert, Barbara Westergaard and David Hicks. "The Structure of Design Firms in the Construction Industry." *Environment and Planning B,* 4 (1977), pp. 3-29.

Herdeg, Klaus. *The Decorated Diagram.* Cambridge, Mass.: Harvard University Press, 1983.

Hillebrandt, Patricia M. *Economic Theory and the Construction Industry.* London: Macmillan, 1974.

Hirsch, Ruth. "Management: The Market for Architects." *Progressive Architecture,* 67, no. 7 (July 1986), pp. 63-68.

"Hot New Market Lures A-E Players to Cutting Edge." *Engineering News Record,* April 4, 1985, pp. 30-32.

"Insurance up 33 Percent in One Year." *Architectural Technology,* July/August 1986, p. 23.

Jacques Cattell Press. *American Art Directory,* 1984. 50th ed. New York: R.R. Bowker, 1985.

Jenkins, Frank. *Architect and Patron.* London: Oxford University Press, 1961.

Kidder, Tracy. *House.* Boston: Houghton Mifflin, 1985.

Kieran, Stephen. "The Architecture of Plenty: Theory and Design in the Marketing Age." *Harvard Architecture Review: Patronage,* 6, pp. 102-13.

Kimmel, Peter S. "The Facility Management Market." *Architectural Technology,* July/August 1986, pp. 44-53.

Kotschnig, Walter M. *Unemployment in the Learned Professions.* London: Oxford University Press, 1937.

Landau, Sarah B. *Edward T. and William A. Potter: American Victorian Architects.* New York: Garland Publishing, 1979.

Lange, Julian E. and D. Quinn Mills. *The Construction Industry: Balance Wheel of the Economy.* Lexington, Mass.: Lexington Books, 1979.

Lapidus, Morris. *Architecture: A Profession and a Business.* New York: Reinhold Publishing, 1967.

Larson, Magali Sarfatti. "Emblem and Exception: The Historical Definition of the Architect's Professional Role." In Blau, LaGory, and Pipkin, eds., *Professionals and Urban Form,* chap. 2.

—. *The Rise of Professionalism: A Sociological Analysis.* Berkeley: University of California Press, 1974.

Larson, Magali Sarfatti, George Leon, and Jay Bolick. "The Professional Supply of Design: A Descriptive Study of Architectural Firms." In Blau, La Gory and, Pipkin, eds., *Professionals and Urban Form,* chap. 10.

Levy, Richard. *The Professionalization of American Architects and Civil Engineers, 1865-1917.* Ann Arbor, Mich.: University Microfilms, 1980.

Lewis, Roger K.. *Architect?* Cambridge, Mass.: MIT Press, 1985.

MacDonald, Stephen. "Building Battle: Interior Designers Pitted against Architects in Licensing Dispute." *Wall Street Journal,* May 6, 1987, p. 33.

Maister, David H. "Lessons in Client-Loving." *Architectural Technology,* Fall 1985, pp. 47-49.

—. "Profitability: Beating the Downward Trend." *Journal of Management Consulting,* 1, no. 4 (Fall 1984), pp. 39-44.

Mark, Robert. *Experiments in Gothic Architecture.* Cambridge, Mass.: MIT Press, 1982.

McCue, Gerald M. and William R. Ewald, Jr. *Creating the Human Environment.* Urbana: University of Illinois Press, 1970.

McElroy, Martin. "How Big Corporations Choose Design Firms." *Architectural Record,* 172, no. 6 (June 1984), pp. 45-47.

McEwen, Malcolm. *Crisis in Architecture.* London: RIBA Publications, 1974.

Meyer, Karl E. *The Art Museum: Power, Money, Ethics.* New York: William Morrow, 1979.

Misner, Christopher K. "The A-Ds, Architect-Developers: Types and Possibilities" Senior thesis, Princeton University School of Architecture, 1987.

"Mt. Sinai's Multimedia Campaign." *New York Times,* February 24, 1987, p. D23.

Nuffield Foundation. Division for Architectural Studies. *The Design of Research Laboratories.* London: Oxford University Press, 1961.

Nydele, Ann. "Practice: Comes the Facilities Manager." *Architectural Record,* 173, no. 6 (May 1985), pp. 51-53 and no. 7 (June 1985), pp. 47-53.

Oberlender, Garold B. "Development of Construction Research." *Journal of Construction Engineering and Management,* 110, no. 4 (December 1984), pp. 486-90.

Owings, Nathaniel. *The Spaces In Between: An Architect's Journey.* Boston: Houghton Mifflin, 1973.

"One in Five Owners Hire CM First, Survey Shows." *Building Design and Construction,* 20, no. 2 (February 1979), p. 35.

Phillippo, Gene. *The Professional Guide to Real Estate Development.* Homewood, Ill.: Dow Jones-Irwin, 1976.

Piore, Michael and Charles Sabel. *The Second Industrial Divide: Possibilities for Prosperity.* New York: Basic Books, 1984.

Portman, John and Jonathan Barnett. *The Architect as Developer.* New York: McGraw-Hill, 1976.

"Practice: What Can We Do about the Liability Crisis Now?". *Architectural Record,* 174, no. 7 (June 1986), pp. 35-39.

Saint, Andrew. *The Image of the Architect.* New Haven: Yale University Press, 1983.

Schluntz, Roger. "Alternative Careers of Architectural Graduates." *Crit 8,* Fall 1980, pp. 18-20.

Schuman, Tony. "Professionalism and Social Goals of Architects, 1930-1980." In Paul L. Knox, ed., *The Design Professions and the Built Environment.* Beckenham, England: Croom Helm, 1987.

Schwartz, Bonnie F. *The Civil Works Administration, 1933-1934.* Princeton, N.J.: Princeton University Press, 1985.

Sennewald, Bea. "Smart Buildings: Facts, Myths and Implications." *Architectural Technology,* March/April 1986, pp. 21-35.

Smyth, Hedley. *Property Companies and the Construction Industry in Great Britain.* Cambridge: Cambridge University Press, 1985.

Society for Marketing Professional Services. *Distinguished Paper Series 1986.*

Stanback, Thomas M., Jr., et al. *Services: The New Economy.* Totowa: Allanheld, Osmun and Co., 1981.

"Straight Talk from Straight Folks: America's Marketing Leaders Speak." *SMPS News,* 12, no. 2 (February 1987), pp. 3-4.

"Survey Indicates Preference for Licensing of CM's." *Building Design and Construction,* February 1979, p. 35.

"Survey on Architect Selection Revealed." *Architectural Record,* 173, no. 8 (July 1985), p. 33.

"Survival in a Down Market: Lessons from the Past." *SMPS News,* 12, no. 4 (April 1987), pp. 1 and 5.

Sweet, Justin. *Legal Aspects of Architecture, Engineering and the Construction Process.* 3d ed. St. Paul, Minn.: West Publishing Co., 1985.

Swinburne, Herbert. *Design Cost Analysis.* New York: McGraw-Hill, 1980.

"The 200 Architectural Giants of 1986." Corporate Design and Realty, 5, no. 8 (September 1986), p. 38-49.

Van Rensselaer, Mariana G. "Client and Architect." In Lewis Mumford, ed., *The Roots of American Architecture.* New York: Reinhold Publishing, 1952, pp. 260-68.

Ventre, Francis. "Building in Eclipse." *Progressive Architecture,* 63, no. 12 (December 1982), pp. 57-59.

—. "Myth and Paradox in the Building Enterprise." In Paul L. Knox, ed., *The Design Professions and the Built Environment.* Beckenham, England: Croom Helm, 1987.

Warszawski, Abraham. "Formal Education in Construction Management." *Journal of the Construction Division, Proceedings of the American Society of Civil Engineers,* 98, no. CO 2 (September 1972), pp. 251-55.

Wills, Royal Barry. *The Business of Architecture.* New York: Reinhold Publishing, 1941.

Wineman, Jean D., ed. *Behavioral Issues in Office Design.* New York: Van Nostrand Reinhold, 1986.

Wright, John W. *American Almanac of Jobs and Salaries.* New York: Avon Books, 1982.

Zukin, Sharon. *Loft Living: Culture and Capital in Urban Change.* Baltimore: The Johns Hopkins University Press, 1982.

Government Sources

United Nations. Economic Commission for Europe. *Annual Bulletin of Housing and Building Statistics for Europe.* Geneva: Economic Commission for Europe, 1961.

U.S. Department of Commerce, Bureau of the Census. *Census of Population, 1960: Subject Reports, Occupation by Industry.* Washington, D.C.: Government Printing Office, 1963.

—. *Census of Population, 1970: Subject Reports, Occupation by Industry.* Washington, D.C.: Government Printing Office, 1972.

—. *Census of Population, 1980: Subject Reports, Occupation by Industry.* Washington, D.C.: Government Printing Office, 1984.

—. *Census of Selected Services: Architectural and Engineering Firms, 1967.* Washington, D.C.: Government Printing Office, 1970.

—. *Census of Selected Services, 1972.* Washington, D.C.: Government Printing Office, 1976.

—. *Census of Service Industries, 1977.* Washington, D.C.: Government Printing Office, 1981.

—. *Census of Service Industries, 1982.* Washington, D.C.: Government Printing Office, 1985.

—. *Census of the Construction Industries.* Washington, D.C.: Government Printing Office, 1967, 1972, 1977, and 1982.

—. *Statistical Abstract of the United States, 1985.* Washington, D.C.: Government Printing Office, 1984.

—. *Statistical Abstract of the United States, 1986.* Washington, D.C.: Government Printing Office, 1985.

U.S. Department of Labor, Bureau of Labor Statistics. "The Job Outlook in Brief." *Occupational Outlook Quarterly,* 26, no.1 (Spring 1982), pp. 9-13.

U.S. General Services Administration, Office of Design and Construction. *Architect/Engineer Services.* Washington, D.C.: G.S.A., February 1984.

U.S. House of Representatives, Hearing before the Subcommittee on Public Buildings and Grounds, July 1, 1979. *Public Building Needs.* Washington, D.C.: U.S. Government Printing Office, 1979.

U.S. Senate, Hearing before the Committee on the Environment and Public Works, October 15, 1979. *Architectural Competitions.* Washington, D.C.: U.S. Government Printing Office, 1979.

Journals and Newspapers

AIA Journal
Architectural Record
Architectural Technology
Building Design and Construction
Business Week
Construction Review
Corporate Design and Realty
Engineering News Record (ENR)
Environmental Design Research News
Facilities
Facility Management News
Memo
National Law Journal
New York Times
Progressive Architecture
Royal Institute of British Architects Journal
SMPS News
Wall Street Journal

Index

COLOPHON

This book was designed and produced by Elizabeth Short and Kevin Lippert. The typeface is Bitstream Charter, designed by Matthew Carter; the type was set by Desktop Publishing of San Rafael, California. Like all Princeton Architectural Press books, *Architectural Practice* is printed on acid-free paper, which will not yellow, and bound to insure that the pages will not fall out.